MIGRANTS UNDER SIEGE

WRITTEN BY:

PRINCE EWEMADE KONKONS

Edited BY:

PRINCE EWEMADE KONKONS

©

Dynasty Prince Books Publishers

A publication by Dynasty Prince Books Publisher.

© Dynasty Prince Books Publisher 2024

First published 2022

ISBN: 9798305149852

Printed and published in Nigeria by:

Dynasty Prince books Publisher

Edo State, Nigeria

Tel: +2348026233860

ISBN: 9798305149852

DEDICATION

The book is dedicated to all African descent who have shown remarkable resilience in their ongoing fight against oppression and systemic discrimination found in various institutions, schools, and workplaces outside their home countries. This dedication especially honours those who have faced significant challenges, including threats to their lives, dehumanization, and psychological suffering caused by those in authority, yet have remained steadfast in their determination.

CONTENTS

DEDICATION

ABOUT THE BOOK

AUTHOR BIOGRAPHY

CHAPTER ONE – HOME AWAY FROM HOME

CHAPTER TWO - BEGININING OF TIME

CHPATER THREE- JOURNEY

CHAPTER FOUR - REAL LIFE

CHAPTER FIVE- STRUGGLE

CHAPTER SIX- SYTEMATIC DISTRIMINATION

CHAPTER SEVEN- NEVER GIVE UP

CHAPTER EIGHT- IT IS THE SAME CRY IN EVERY COUNTRY

CHAPTER NINE- GLOBAL INJUSTICE AGAINST MIGRANTS AND THEIR CHILDREN

CHAPTER TEN- OVERCOMING THE STRUGGLE AS MIGRANTS

CHAPTER ELEVEN- UNDERSTANDING MIGRATION TRAJECTORIES

CHAPTER TWELVEN- - DYNAMIC MOTIVATION AND SHIFTING DESTINATIONS

CHAPTER THIRTEEN- TWO MEANING OF TRAJECTORY

CHAPTER FOURTEEN- BIGGEST CHALLENGE FACING MIGRANTS

CHAPTER FIFTEEN- ECONOMIC AND SOCIAL IMPACT OF MIGRANT

CHAPTER SIXTEEN- COMPARE AND CONTRAST THE ADVANTAGES AND DISADVANTAGE OF MIGRANTS

CHAPTER SEVENTEEN- HEROS PAST

CHAPTER EIGHTEEN- HEROES OF TODAY

CHAPTER NINETEEN- AUTHORS RECOMMEDATIONS

ABOUT THE BOOK

"Migrants Under Siege" offers a thorough exploration of the challenging experiences migrants face in Western countries. The author presents personal narratives that shed light on the obstacles many migrants encounter within a system that professes to uphold democratic values, emphasizing the systemic discrimination they suffer. This discrimination is intensified by a deliberate effort to marginalize migrants, which gradually undermines their spirit and resilience.

The book provides numerous examples of marginalization, particularly affecting African migrants from various cities and countries worldwide. It represents a significant contribution by weaving historical context with compelling storytelling, delivering a powerful narrative grounded in real-life experiences. These stories prompt readers to reflect on pressing issues while also nurturing hope for future generations of Africans. It is vital for these individuals to seek liberation from corrupt elites in their home countries, who intentionally perpetuate suffering and chaos, leaving them with few options but to pursue a better life abroad. However, this journey often takes a heavy emotional toll, resulting in deep sorrow.

PROLOGUE:
(MENTAL FLIGHT)

As a young boy growing up in Benin City, I was often inspired by the many talented Nigerian youths who excelled in various international sports competitions, including boxing, wrestling, judo, karate, handball, and other sports available at that time. However, the current generation of youths faces a markedly different reality.

I find myself pondering what has transpired in the largest nation of Black people, often referred to as the giant of Africa. I question what transgressions we, as a nation, may have committed that seem to have led to divine neglect.

Like other nights, I woke up around 2-3 AM, contemplating the current situation in Nigeria, Africa, and indeed the world. However, this night felt different. At around 2 AM local time in Sweden, I lay in my modest but comfortable bed, reflecting on what we, as the youth of this generation, could do to improve the dire situation in Nigeria and Africa. Answers eluded me, so I embarked on a mental journey back to Nigeria and the African continent.

My first stop was my birthplace, Edo State, where I assessed the current circumstances. I recalled the former APC National Chairperson, whose promises

during the 2015 general elections included reducing the exchange rate of the US dollar to one Naira and implementing much-needed reforms for Nigerians. Next, I visited the Palace of His Royal Majesty, my beloved king and our royal father, Omo N'Oba N'Edo, Uku Akpolokpolo, Ewuare II, Ogididgan, Oba of Benin, who has made significant contributions to his people in a brief time. Long may he reign.
Continuing my mental journey, I travelled through Asaba, the capital of Delta State, and further on to Minna, Niger State, the birthplace of the IBB who Nigerians alleged undermined democracy in Nigeria and oversaw the emergence of 4.1.9. I pressed on to Katsina State, the home of President Bubi where I was struck by the stark realities I encountered.
I began to grasp the reasons behind the widespread hunger in the land and the siege under which Nigerians currently live. My journey took me through Northern States to the Palace of the Sultan of Sokoto, where I sought to understand the situation better. I then ventured into the western states, passing through Ogun State, home to a former civilian and military president who had every opportunity to effect positive change in Nigeria but failed.

I continued to Lagos State, where I witnessed the tangible evidence of democracy in action. I thought to myself that if all political leaders could adopt the mindset of former Lagos State Governor Fashola and the current governor, Ambode, our nation would be in a much better position. My mental flight then took me to the nation's capital, Abuja, navigating through the green and red chambers, where the nation's leadership seems increasingly fragmented. I mused that if divine intervention were to occur today, these chambers might become obsolete, paving the way for true federalism.

My journey did not end there; I travelled to Cape Town, South Africa, where I observed the tragic violence against Nigerians and the mistreatment by South African police. I continued to Libya, where I witnessed the horrific and inhumane treatment inflicted upon Nigerians and other African youths. My mental flight took me to Kuala Lumpur, Malaysia, where young men resort to scamming as a means of survival, and then to Bangkok, Thailand, where Nigerians face death sentences for drug-related offenses.

I also ventured to Brussels, the heart of Europe, where I saw young Africans resorting to prostitution to make ends meet. My journey continued to Reno, Nevada, where I observed police disproportionately targeting Black individuals in luxury vehicles, a phenomenon known as "Driving While Black." I then travelled to Tasmania, Australia, where the Indigenous population lives in extreme poverty, despite the nation's wealth, and Black individuals face systemic disrespect.

I did not stop there; my mental journey led me to

Sweden, where I witnessed the harsh realities faced by migrants, a nation that suppresses their voices and seeks to silence anyone who dares to speak out against the injustices faced by African migrants. I then travelled to the United Kingdom, the cradle of Western civilization. I first visited Buckingham Palace, where I hold hope that King Charles will bring about meaningful change. In London, I observed grieving migrant parents mourning the loss of a teenage boy to a stabbing. My journey took me to Glasgow, Scotland, where young men of African descent murdered, their bodies discarded without accountability for the four Black victims.
Eventually, I returned from my mental flight to my bed, holding onto the hope that one day, a revolutionary leader will emerge—someone willing to pay the ultimate price for the freedom of our people, ready to liberate Nigerian youths and Africans from their current plight, which includes prostitution, drowning at sea, drug dealing, emotional suffering, and the depression stemming from their so-called comfort zones in Western nations, where they work 15-hour shifts just to provide for their families.
I hope that this generation can pass on a much better Nigeria and Africa to the next. I am Prince Ewemade Konkons, and I yearn for a brighter future for all in Nigeria and Africa.

AUTHOR BIOGRAPHY

Prince Ewemade Konkons is a dedicated Christian and a devoted father. He holds the esteemed position of Public Relations Officer for the Global Coalition for Security and Democracy in Nigeria (GCSDN) and serves as the Executive Director for both Avossia and Nosakhare Nig Ltd. Additionally, he is the founder of dynastyprincebooks.com and the President and founder of the Aimien and Abina Foundation (A&A).

A multifaceted individual, Prince Ewemade Konkons embodies various roles, including comrade, writer, human rights activist, critical thinker, and advocate for the people. Driven by a revolutionary mindset, he strives to make a positive impact on society.

Prince Ewemade began his professional journey in the United States as specialized security personnel. He earned an Associate of Applied Science (AAS) in Computer Information Technology from the prestigious Community College of Southern Nevada. He further pursued a Level 6 Health and Social Care Management qualification, equivalent to a BSc, from the renowned London School of Economics. Currently, he is working towards an LLB in Law at the Open University in Milton Keynes. In addition, he has obtained a Level 7 Strategic Management and Leadership Diploma, along with several other diplomas. On December 12, 2023, he was awarded an Honorary Doctorate Degree in Human Resource Management by The Rescue Mission Theological University USA.

Beyond his passion for writing, Prince Ewemade Konkons explores untold stories, historical accounts, and momentous events. His goal is to pave the way for future generations of Nigerians and Africans through his literary contributions.

His early education marked by success, beginning at the esteemed RDC Nursery School in the affluent Government Reservation Area of Benin City, followed by Emotan Primary School in the same city. He completed his high school education at the renowned Edo College in Benin. Prince Ewemade actively encourages Africans to embrace and share their narratives in their authentic voices.

Hailing from Benin City in Edo State, Nigeria, Prince Ewemade Konkons is the first in his family to pursue a career in writing. He embarked on this journey after his 50th birthday with his book titled "The Sojourn of an African Child." Since then, he has published Various works, including "The Refugee Project," which was released in conjunction with World Refugee Day on June 20, 2022. Other notable titles include "Migrants Under Siege," "The Ungrateful Friends," "Crime and Criminality Expose," "Trapped Between Two Nations," "Broken Genealogy," "A Step-by-Step Approach to Legal Emigration from Africa," "My Ghost Will Haunt You," and "Identifying the Qualities of an Admirable Woman."

Born on January 19, 1972, in what was formerly known as Bendel, now Edo State, Nigeria, Prince Ewemade Konkons grew up in a close-knit community where everyone knew one another. He completed his primary and secondary education in Nigeria before embarking on what he refers to as his "sojourner's journey."

CHAPTER ONE
HOME AWAY FROM HOME

"Home away from home represents a significant transition for all migrants navigating life in a foreign land. When we leave our homeland for another country—whether driven by political, social, or economic factors, or in pursuit of educational opportunities—we inevitably undergo profound changes. Our lifestyles and cultural practices are altered, as we adapt to a new social order that may feel entirely alien, particularly for Africans. This transition compels us to rethink our perspectives and adjust our reasoning to align with the norms of our unfamiliar environment. Morally, we find ourselves with little choice but to adapt.

For individuals living away from home, the experience can be particularly challenging. However, for those who migrate with family, the journey may be easier, as there is a support system in place for emotional and practical assistance.

The first step in this journey involves integrating into the local system, a process that demands considerable time, energy, and resilience, whether through seeking asylum, marriage, or educational opportunities. Each of these pathways presents its own set of mental and physical challenges. Navigating the complexities of immigration offices to secure legal status in your new home can be particularly stressful. Throughout this process, one may encounter various irregularities. As asylum seekers, you might face significant hurdles, while those marrying citizens may experience fewer obstacles. Conversely, individuals seeking settlement through education might find the process less fraught.

The degree of marginalization within the system remains consistent, regardless of the method of integration. This marginalization is often deeply entrenched, existing long before your arrival. Systematic discrimination appears designed to keep people of colour in what I would describe as a state of siege. This phenomenon is pervasive, affecting every aspect of life—from your children's daycare and primary school to higher education institutions. While young children may be oblivious to these dynamics, parents often become. acutely aware of the challenges as they interact with various governmental agencies responsible for managing daily affairs.

In summary, it is my belief that all migrants find themselves 'under siege' in some form."

CHAPTER TWO
BEGININING OF TIME

Many nations hold a condescending view of migrants of African descent, whether intentionally or not. Africans were born into their identity not by choice, but by a shared destiny; God created them as Africans, just as He created the peoples of the Middle East, Asia, North America, and Europe. None of this was a matter of choice or chance, but a part of a common destiny.

Discrimination against individuals based solely on differing values, cultural backgrounds, or misguided assumptions about the worth of Africans is unjustifiable. It is essential to recognize that Africans do not require leftovers to survive. They are not impoverished, nor are they hungry; they are not animals, as some may mistakenly believe. They are not criminals, nor are they akin to baboons or chimpanzees caged in a zoo in Sub-Saharan Africa.

The circumstances facing Africans today are a result of actions taken by individuals like them—greedy individuals who were installed in power following the end of colonization. The suffering endured by Africans is a direct consequence of the foundations laid by your ancestors during their invasions and colonization. Much was taken from our people, particularly our valuables, through slavery and colonization.

Our lineage has seen the dispersal of slaves across the globe—from Europe to North America and the Caribbean. Our ancestors significantly contributed to the development of Western nations' success stories. The world powers of today owe their status to the hard work, dedication, and sacrifices of the plantation workers who came before us. They built the roads and bridges that connect major capitals around the world. Many nations' achievements would not have been possible without the sacrifices of African slaves. Our presence on the soil of most nations should be celebrated as a testament to humanity.

A special place should be reserved for all descendants of African slaves in every nation's capital, wherever they choose to reside. African ancestors have paid the price in full, and Africans deserve to be treated with dignity and respect, despite the challenges imposed upon them from various nations in Africa. They have enabled many Western nations' generations to enjoy the luxuries of today. Evidence suggests that they continue to be the primary beneficiaries of Africa's collective wealth in the twenty-first century. How can the continent be free when citizens of Western nations continue to exploit African nations through backdoor dealings?

Africans deserve a level of respect in all Western nations. It is crucial to educate the younger generations of Western nations and their people about history, as it seems that many have quickly forgotten the events that transpired between their nations and the African continent. Africans have chosen to seek and speak the truth, regardless of how uncomfortable it may sound to Western nations and their citizens. African voices must be heard.

CHAPTER THREE
JOURNEY

The experiences of migrants of African descent remain strikingly similar, regardless of where they find themselves—whether in Australia, Japan, Europe, the United Kingdom, or Ireland, with the United States being a notable exception that I will elaborate on later.

Migrants often encounter systemic discrimination that permeates various aspects of life, from the immigration process to employment, education, and healthcare, affecting both young and old. There exists a barrier, whether intentional or not, that hinders the progress of migrants of African descent. This discrimination extends to their children as well, who are not spared from the systemic biases in place.

In the Netherlands, for instance, there is unambiguous evidence of structural disadvantages and systematic discrimination against minority African migrants. Their participation in the workforce significantly lags that of native Dutch citizens, often relegating them to undesirable jobs that most Dutch individuals would not consider. This results in a stagnation that makes upward mobility impossible, while regression is not an option.

Many African migrants endure their struggles in silence, as no government agency in this region appears immune to these discriminatory practices. The children of migrants also face educational discrimination, often being pushed toward vocational training instead of university education, particularly when they exhibit hyperactive behaviours in school. These children are frequently diagnosed with attention deficit hyperactivity disorder (ADHD), a label that complicates their pursuit of higher education.

Migrants of African descent encounter numerous challenges, ranging from housing issues to social integration. They often adapt to these adversities, feeling they have no alternative but to confront them as they arise. In various parts of the Western world, African migrants find themselves under siege, judged primarily by the colour of their skin rather than their character. It is essential to recognize that no individual should be assessed based on their skin colour. Indeed, it is a fundamental truth that all individuals are created equal, irrespective of race, hair colour, or eye colour.

CHAPTER FOUR
REAL-LIFE

The law enacted by Papal Bull in 1452 remains valid today in many European capitals. This law permitted European nations to treat individuals whose faith was not Roman Catholic as property. The Papal Bulls were subsequently integrated into the legal frameworks of various European countries, including Portugal, Spain, England, France, Belgium, and the Netherlands. As a result, anyone not classified as European faced numerous limitations, restrictions, and barriers across all nations under European control. This situation persisted for centuries and continues to be relevant today.

While the UK abolished the slave trade in 1807 and ended the enslavement of Black individuals in the British Empire in 1834, and although British political control over most of its African and Caribbean colonies concluded in the 1960s, the repercussions of the injustices initiated in 1452 by Pope Nicholas V still linger. People of African descent continue to endure limitations and barriers that hinder their progress and social mobility in Western nations, particularly in European cities and countries.

The ongoing issue can be attributed to a long-standing moral detachment that has led many Europeans to treat non-Europeans unjustly. We believe that laws lacking effective enforcement will be disregarded. Consequently, in 2022, we witness this troubling behaviour in numerous European countries, including the UK. We contend that systemic racism and the marginalization of migrants can be eradicated, but this change will only occur with the robust enforcement of existing laws that convey a clear message: morally reprehensible behaviour will no longer be tolerated in our society.

The killing of George Floyd on May 25, 2020, shocked viewers worldwide and ignited protests by the Black Lives Matter movement in the USA, the UK, and beyond, involving individuals of all ethnicities and ages. These protests represented an "alliance of conscience," a collective of fair-minded individuals advocating for societal change and a departure from the morally reprehensible behaviour that has adversely affected citizens of African descent for far too long. We believe that Africans should be treated differently, and this "alliance of conscience" can drive the necessary transformation. Reach Society envisions the 21st century as the era when the systemic racism and migrant persecution initiated in 1452 will be dismantled, as decent people of all backgrounds refuse to tolerate the morally abhorrent actions of the past.

Furthermore, the contemporary African community must educate its youth about this historical timeline of systemic racism. Young people should learn that the abuse and persecution of individuals of African descent by Europeans originated from the malevolent actions of Pope Nicholas V and were perpetuated for centuries by colonial powers. Despite recent legislation against racial discrimination, meaningful behavioural change among employers, institutions, and service providers is slow due to inadequate enforcement by governments.

As a result, individuals of European descent often feel free to continue their ingrained discriminatory practices, obstructing the development and progress of people of African heritage.

It is essential for the modern African community to instil in its youth the belief that they possess the potential to realize their dreams and lead fulfilling, meaningful lives. From an early age, they must be taught to reject any narrative—whether from family, friends, or strangers—that suggests they are inferior due to their skin colour or ethnicity. Such notions have never been true and will never be true. In the 21st century, scientific advancements have demonstrated that all human beings share the same genetic makeup, regardless of ethnicity.

Thus, parents of African descent must invest in their children from birth, nurturing and preparing them to thrive in our qualification-driven society. This involves encouraging a love for reading bedtime stories and fostering an affinity for mathematics by mastering multiplication tables. Parents should engage their children in discussions about literature and societal events, helping them develop critical thinking skills on a wide range of topics. Additionally, young people should frequently utilize the Internet to expand their general knowledge.

The quote, "What we do in life echoes in eternity," spoken by General Maximus in the film Gladiator, resonates deeply. The actions of Pope Nicholas V in 1452 have reverberated throughout history for 570 years. In the 21st century, we could mitigate the impact of this historical injustice by carefully considering what we communicate to our youth. By doing so, we can inoculate them against the trauma of systemic racism, bolster their resilience, and empower them to shape their futures.

Today, we believe that leaders within the modern African community must prioritize this inoculation process, ensuring that our actions will also "echo in eternity." People of African descent face systemic racism in Europe, as highlighted in the report "Being Black in the EU," which confirmed that Black individuals experience higher levels of discrimination than the general European population. There is unmistakable evidence that being Black in the EU entails enduring systemic racism and discrimination in employment, wages, housing, and healthcare.

Addressing these issues requires a multifaceted approach, including educating European children about their countries' colonial histories and training law enforcement agencies to recognize and eliminate racist behaviours. In the 21st century, there is no justification for racial discrimination.

In some countries, up to 76% of young people of African descent are neither employed nor engaged in education or training, compared to just 8% of the general population. Additionally, 14% of respondents reported that private landlords refused to rent to them, and only 15% of individuals of African descent owned their homes, compared to 70% of the overall EU population.

Moreover, individuals facing multiple forms of discrimination, such as Black people and migrants in certain Italian communities, often encounter physical and verbal attacks as part of their daily lives, as reported by Targeted Toward Refugees. The stress stemming from this climate of hostility adversely affects the mental and physical health of Black individuals living in Europe, a concern that has been overlooked by those in positions of authority.

CHAPTER FIVE
STRUGGLE

The African continent is now widely acknowledged as the birthplace of humanity and the cradle of civilization. We continue to be in awe of the remarkable achievements of Kemet, or Ancient Egypt, which is one of the most notable early African civilizations that emerged in the Nile Valley over 5,000 years ago.

Even prior to the rise of Kemet, it is likely that an even more ancient kingdom, known as Ta Seti, existed in what is now Nubia in Sudan. This kingdom may have been the earliest state to exist anywhere in the world. Therefore, Africa can be credited not only with the scientific advancements associated with Egypt—such as engineering, mathematics, architecture, and medicine—but also with significant early political developments, including state formation and monarchy. This evidence suggests that, during this ancient period, economic, political, and scientific development in Africa may have been more advanced than in other continents.

The African continent continued its own trajectory of development with minimal external interference until the fifteenth century. Other great civilizations, such as Kush, Axum, Mali, and Great Zimbabwe, flourished in Africa before 1500. During this early period, Africans engaged in extensive international trade networks and trans-oceanic travel. Notably, some African states established important trading relationships with India, China, and other parts of Asia long before these connections were disrupted by European intervention.

In the 8th century, a North African conquest of the Iberian Peninsula commenced, leading to the occupation of much of Spain and Portugal for several centuries. This Muslim invasion reintroduced much of the ancient world's knowledge to Europe and strengthened its ties with North and West Africa. The wealth generated from the great empires of West Africa, such as Ghana, Mali, and Songhay, fuelled Europe's economic expansion in the 13th and 14th centuries and piqued European interest in western Africa. Indeed, it was the riches of West Africa, particularly its gold, which inspired the voyages of early European explorers.

By the 15th century, the African continent was characterized by significant diversity. The existence of powerful kingdoms and empires, such as Mali in the west and Ethiopia in the east, was more the exception than the rule. In many regions, no major centralized states existed, and many people lived in societies with minimal wealth and power disparities.

In such societies, governance often took the form of more democratic systems led by councils of elders

and other kinship and age-based institutions. Consequently, there was a rich diversity of religious and philosophical beliefs, many of which remained traditional and emphasized the importance of connecting with ancestors. The Ethiopian kingdom was distinctive in that the Orthodox Christian church, which has ancient roots in the region, played increasingly significant state roles. In Mali and other areas of western and eastern Africa, as well as throughout North Africa, Islam had begun to exert a notable influence before 1500. Most importantly, African societies were following their own developmental patterns prior to European intervention.

In the 18th century, racist perspectives on Africa were most famously articulated by Scottish philosopher David Hume, who expressed suspicion that Black individuals were naturally inferior to Whites, claiming that there had never been a civilized nation of that complexion. While some views evolved over time, others persisted. In the 19th century, German philosopher Hegel declared, "Africa is no historical part of the world." Later, Hugh Trevor-Roper, Regius Professor of History at Oxford University, openly stated the racist belief that Africa has no history, a sentiment echoed as recently as 1963.

We now understand that far from lacking a history, Africa is certainly the cradle of human history. All the earliest evidence of human existence and our immediate hominid ancestors has been discovered in Africa. Recent scientific research indicates that all human beings share African ancestry.

Africa was not only the birthplace of humanity but also the cradle of early civilizations that made immense contributions to the world and continue to be admired today. Kemet, the original name of ancient Egypt, is a prime example, having first emerged in the Nile Valley over 5,000 years ago as one of the earliest monarchies.

However, even before Egypt's rise, an earlier kingdom was established in Nubia, in present-day Sudan. Ta Seti is believed to be one of the earliest states in history, illustrating that thousands of years ago, Africans were developing some of the most advanced political systems in the world.

Between the 7th and 15th centuries, the external Muslim demand for African goods also included a demand for captives. Forms of slavery have existed on all continents at various times in history, often as a means of exploiting those captured in war, particularly in regions facing labour shortages alongside abundant land. Slavery was indeed present in some African societies before the advent of Islam. For instance, ancient Kemet records describe European slaves being branded. Later, in other powerful African

states, enslaved individuals or those who were unfree could be found, although their status often resembled that of impoverished farmers. This situation may have been akin to that of serfs in medieval Europe, who were obligated to produce agricultural surpluses or fulfil other duties for a specific ruler.

However, when external demand for enslaved individuals emerged, some African societies were able to and did supply slaves. For example, there was an export "trade" in enslaved people, transporting them via the Sahara from West to North Africa, following routes like those used for other trade goods like gold and salt. Enslaved Africans were also forcibly taken to parts of the Middle East, India, and even as far as China. One of the most renowned slaves of East African origin is Malik Ambar (1549–1626), who was born in present-day Ethiopia. Enslaved at a youthful age, he eventually became the regent of the Indian kingdom of Ahmednagar, known for his military campaigns against the Mughals.

The development of states in Africa contributed to increased levels of inequality—between men and women, the rich and the poor, and the free and the unfree. In fact, inequality and economic exploitation were particularly pronounced in some of the most powerful and developed states, such as the Ethiopian kingdom. Historians regard Ethiopia as a feudal society, characterized by features similar to those of

feudalism in Europe, where economic and political power was derived from land ownership and the exploitation of those compelled to work that land. Are we still beholden to colonial masters even after the abolition of slavery?

CHAPTER SIX
SYSTEMATIC DISCRIMINATION

Over 200 million individuals of African descent reside in the United States, with millions more living in various regions around the globe, outside of the African continent. Whether as descendants of those affected by the transatlantic slave trade or as more recent migrants, they represent some of the most impoverished and marginalized communities worldwide.

For centuries, people of African descent have faced marginalization because of slavery and colonialism. There is a growing consensus that systemic racism and racial discrimination have hindered their progress in numerous aspects of public life. These communities have endured exclusion and poverty, often remaining "invisible" in official statistics. While there has been some progress, the challenges persist to varying degrees in many parts of the world, particularly in numerous European cities.

The factors contributing to poverty among people of African descent are primarily structural. Discrimination manifests in the unequal

access these groups have to essential services. For instance, individuals of African descent often face disadvantages in accessing education, healthcare, markets, loans, and technology. The discrimination they encounter has intensified, as Western nations frequently overlook the contributions of African migrants in favour of nationals from Arab-speaking countries. The interests of Arab-speaking individuals are often prioritized over those of Africans, particularly Nigerians, who are frequently marginalized in employment opportunities.

The treatment of African migrants is often derogatory, as highlighted by the remarks of the President of the United States. Despite preaching peace and prosperity to the international community, Western nations often exhibit a double standard, portraying themselves as accessible and tolerant while treating marginalized groups poorly.

The discrimination faced by African migrants warrants greater attention from Western nations, which are often the perpetrators of these injustices. Laws that discriminate against non-nationals, coupled with programs and policies that fail to address their specific needs and vulnerabilities, frequently result in migrants and their families being unable to access basic services or only being able to do so at levels that do not meet international human rights standards. Issues related to the employment of economic, social, and cultural rights are particularly critical for many migrants, who often encounter severe discrimination in housing, education, healthcare, employment, and social security.

African migrants continue to face significant challenges in every city and country across the Western world, including barriers to employment, housing, and daily life, all stemming from laws and systems established by the founding architects of these nations.

We are indeed under siege in various aspects of our daily lives. Our children, born in these Western nations, also face challenges in daycare centres, primary schools, and universities. They encounter difficulties when playing with peers of different races and backgrounds.

It is imperative for global powers to rise to the challenges of the twenty-first century and address this critical issue. They must begin to enact laws that reflect a departure from outdated approaches to African migrants. Systemic discrimination is deeply embedded in the national self-image of many European cities and countries, which, in my view, often practice a form of "racial democracy."

CHAPTER SEVEN
NEVER GIVE UP

"Never give up" is a mantra we hear throughout our lives—from our parents, storybooks, teachers, coaches, mentors, and colleagues. This idealistic philosophy suggests that if we persistently work hard, we will achieve the results we desire. While it may require finding innovative approaches or enhancing our skills to meet challenges, the belief is that perseverance will lead to success.

However, this perspective does not always align with the realities of the world. In many instances, arduous work does lead to success, but it may not be in the form we initially envisioned, nor may it align with our original goals. The truth is that sometimes we must relinquish one objective to pursue another, and occasionally, we need to abandon a less viable idea in favour of a stronger one. Yet, it is equally important to recognize that giving up too soon on a promising idea could mean missing a valuable opportunity.

As migrants of African descent, we share a common DNA—a resilient spirit that drives us to persist in our struggle for equality and justice. We seek a better life than what our parents, families, and friends experienced. Our migration from various African nations is fuelled by similar aspirations: some of us seek a change of environment, others pursue educational opportunities, while many are in search of greener pastures.

Regardless of our origins or religious beliefs, our goals are aligned. Our nations have suffered under the weight of corrupt leadership, often beholden to their colonial masters. These leaders have failed to rectify the injustices faced by their citizens. Despite Africa's wealth of resources that the world relies on, we continue to lag in development, infrastructure, education, and healthcare. There is no denying that Western nations have played a significant role in Africa's underdevelopment.

These circumstances underscore the necessity for Africans to receive the respect and treatment we deserve from host nations. It would be unjust for us to abandon our quest for a fair share of the wealth that has been systematically extracted from our continent and funnelled into Western cities. It would also be a disservice to the millions of enslaved individuals who were forcibly taken from Africa, only to toil in building the infrastructure of countries like Portugal, Spain, France, Great Britain, and the United States. Their descendants now enjoy the luxuries afforded by the sacrifices of our ancestors.

We must remain steadfast in our pursuit of equal and fair treatment, deserving of respect as descendants of those who suffered under slavery.

The leadership of our continent continues to be indirectly influenced by the remnants of colonial rule, more than two hundred years after the abolition of the slave trade. For us, giving up is not an option. We will continue to advocate for the revision and replacement of discriminatory laws that affect migrants of African descent, ensuring they are replaced with fair, just, and equitable standards alongside our white peers.

CHAPTER EIGHT
IT IS THE SAME CRY IN EVERY COUNTRY

In his interview on April 22, 2022, titled "Hope Under Siege," Pope Francis emphasized the plight of millions fleeing their home countries, particularly mothers and children. He cautioned against categorizing refugees and migrants into classes, reminding us that our Lord Jesus was himself a migrant and refugee in Egypt.

We are all migrants in one way or another. If Jesus Christ, the Son of the Creator of the universe, experienced life as a migrant in Egypt, who are we to look down upon individuals based on their race or religion, or to judge them by their appearance or skin colour? We all come from various parts of the world, regardless of our countries of birth or residence.

African migrants, from East to West, North to South, and throughout Central Africa, share a common cry across various cities and countries in the West. They express their anguish over injustice, systemic discrimination, and dehumanization, as if they were less than human. These issues have persisted despite the abolition of slavery over two centuries ago, with laws still actively reinforcing inequality in many non-English-speaking European countries.

For instance, an African graduate in Engineering from Denmark, who achieved a first-class degree, may find himself competing for a job against a white peer with similar qualifications. Yet, while the white candidate secures a directorship, the African migrant may still be searching for employment eight years later, ultimately ending up as a public transit bus driver. Similarly, in Sweden, an African migrant who studied accounting at a prestigious university, graduating with a second-class degree, may still be working as a cleaner seven years later, despite having the same educational background as his peers.

In Germany, an African migrant who studied microbiology finds himself unable to secure a job, while his white counterparts have advanced to senior positions in major tech companies. After ten years, he relocates to the United Kingdom, where he works as

a teacher in a public school. In the Netherlands, children of African migrants are often denied university access due to classifications of hyperactivity disorders. In Madrid, Spain, African migrants are frequently relegated to factory jobs.

The same narrative unfolds in Sydney, Australia, where promotions are often out of reach for African migrants, even when they have superior qualifications compared to their white counterparts. In Dublin, Ireland, aspiring lawyers cannot represent clients in court without the presence of an Irish solicitor. In Italy, African migrants rarely hold key positions, not even as council members.

Indeed, we are all under siege, with few exceptions in the United States, Canada, and Great Britain, each facing its own unique challenges. Unlike in Great Britain, African migrants in Canada can dream big and aspire to reach their goals. While there are still obstacles, they are free to compete with their white counterparts, regardless of their backgrounds. However, 25% of African migrants still struggle to find jobs aligned with their qualifications after four years of university, except for children of African migrants born in Great Britain.

In Canada, opportunities abound for those willing to try. This nation, built on the contributions of migrants from diverse backgrounds, shares similarities with

Great Britain. African migrants are achieving remarkable success, thanks in part to legislative changes that support their advancement. While there is still work to be done, migrants continue to face challenges.

The United States has made significant strides, especially considering its history of slavery. It remains more welcoming to African migrants than many other countries. The shared history between Africa and the United States, particularly with African Americans who were brought as slaves, highlights the contributions of African descendants to the development of the nation. The United States stands as a place where anyone, including African migrants, can aspire to be whatever they choose. It is indeed the land of the free and the home of the brave, especially when led by democratic leaders who open doors of opportunity for people of colour.

However, issues persist regarding race relations between white Americans and African Americans, leading to tragic outcomes for many in the African American community. African migrants receive more respect, dignity, and fairness compared to their experiences in non-English-speaking European countries and other English-speaking nations.

We will remain under siege until every nation revise or amends existing laws that have historically kept

African migrants in bondage, preventing them from excelling in the workplace, in education, and within society. It is imperative that we address this systemic issue for the benefit of future generations of African migrants.

Today, we still find ourselves under siege, just as we did in years past.

CHAPTER NINE

GLOBAL INJUSTICES AGAINST MIGRANTS AND THEIR CHILDREN

African migrants are navigating every corner of the globe in search of greener pastures. They leave the shores of the African continent with a singular goal: to succeed and return to uplift their communities and those they left behind. They endure significant hardships, often relegating themselves to the lowest rungs of society to assimilate into their new environments.

In today's world, migration and global justice rarely align. Although the COVID-19 pandemic temporarily levelled the playing field by drastically limiting international travel, we are now reverting to a status quo where access to safe and legal mobility is grossly uneven. Populations in the Global North, particularly those who are white and affluent, face minimal barriers when crossing international borders.

In contrast, individuals from the Global South, especially those who are black, brown, or poor, encounter substantial, often insurmountable obstacles to migration.

Age also plays a significant role in access to safe and legal mobility. It is, "Against the Best Interests of the Child: The Global Injustice of Migrant Externalization," we argue that children face significant challenges in obtaining necessary protections, partly due to aggressive exclusion policies. These policies include arbitrary detentions of asylum seekers, illegal family separations, and African migrants are navigating every corner of the globe in search of greener pastures.

They leave the shores of the African continent with a singular goal: to succeed and return to uplift their communities and those they left behind. They endure significant hardships, often relegating themselves to the lowest rungs of society to assimilate into their new environments.

Various migration contexts, such as the Mediterranean and Caribbean basins, illustrate the severe impact of these externalization policies on human rights. For instance, children from Nigeria, compelled to leave due to a lack of hope or prospects at home, embark on perilous journeys across Africa to reach Libya as a launching point for migration to Europe. Unfortunately, many of their courageous plans failed in attempting to reach Italy and the EU by crossing the Mediterranean Sea suffer extreme abuse in Libya and face de facto repatriation.

A recent study revealed that 88.2% of young migrants interviewed reported traumatic experiences upon entering Libya, experiences that hindered their ability to reach Italy. The pursuit of a rights-respecting existence in Europe is thwarted not by the children's lack of resilience but by deliberate interference from EU governments and their allies.

Agreements such as the Italy-Libya Memorandum of Understanding from February 2017 are part of a coordinated effort to shield Europe from forced migrants rather than to protect children from harm. These agreements intentionally block escape routes from danger, including those out of Libya and across the Mediterranean, to prevent access to European shores. European governments often justify this interference by citing concerns over threats posed by smugglers, yet the greater danger lies in the obstruction of safe migration pathways.

Consequently, African children seeking access to education, skills training, future employment, and a better life find themselves confined in harsh detention facilities in Libya, with "voluntary return" to Nigeria presented as the only alternative to ongoing incarceration.

An indistinguishable situation unfolds at the external borders of another affluent destination in the Global North. Central American children fleeing violence and other acute threats to their safety encounter stringent externalization measures that obstruct their efforts to seek protection in the United States.

Countries in the so-called Northern Triangle—Honduras, El Salvador, and Guatemala—have become notorious for high rates of violence, with children and youth particularly targeted for abuse, extortion, and other severe human rights violations. These are precisely the circumstances for which international humanitarian protections, including refugee status, were established. Yet, children fleeing such persecution routinely find themselves barred from accessing a safe system to present their asylum claims.

Policies such as the militarization of the US-Mexico border, supported by drones and advanced surveillance technology, alongside the increasing criminalization of irregular border crossings, force families to rely on smugglers, exposing children to riskier journeys and exploitative conditions.

Those who manage to reach the US face punitive measures, including detention, family separation, and protracted asylum processes, while many never cross the border at all.

The COVID-19 pandemic has intensified an already critical human rights crisis at the US southern border. Since 2019, the US government has invoked public health concerns to justify the exclusion of asylum seekers, including families with children, attempting to cross the border to present their claims.

These measures violate international law, which clearly stipulates that such exclusions must be implemented in a non-discriminatory and proportionate manner. Nevertheless, US governments continue to deny extremely vulnerable children and their families access to safety and protection.

We conclude that the real migration crisis is not one of numbers but rather a crisis of solidarity and trust. By externalizing humanitarian responsibilities at the expense of some of the world's most vulnerable children, wealthy Global North nations are exacerbating global injustice rather than promoting global justice.

Countries and regions that have historically prided themselves on their immigrant identities and records of refugee protection are now leading the way in draconian exclusion practices.

While these practices are not new, contemporary strategies for preventing entry have become increasingly far-reaching. Of particular concern for human rights is the rapid expansion of exclusions faced by humanitarian migrants in vulnerable categories, including children.

By shifting the burden of humanitarian responsibility onto poorer neighbouring states, affluent destination countries are complicit in causing egregious harm in two significant ways: first, by denying refugee children and other distressed migrants' access to essential humanitarian protection on their territory, violating binding legal obligations; and second, through the development and proliferation of deliberate deterrent policies, these states are wilfully relegating distressed migrants to regions known for rampant violence and lawlessness.

This chapter will explore the effects of migration externalization on distressed migrant children and their families in both the Mediterranean and Caribbean basins. It will highlight the state-induced obstacles to protection faced by populations seeking refuge in the EU but stranded in Libya, as well as those prevented from seeking protection in the US.

Linguistic and cultural differences, housing costs, and a lack of portability of pension rights across countries can all pose challenges to migration. These challenges often include low wages, inhumane working hours, and hazardous conditions. Newcomers to America frequently encounter barriers such as language difficulties with employers and co-workers, as well as a lack of understanding regarding employment laws that protect workers.

Most immigrants find themselves unemployed and unable to afford housing. Securing accommodation in a new country is extremely challenging, requiring heightened safety measures. Immigrants often face discrimination in the workplace, being excluded from important roles and projects despite their qualifications. No matter how one examines the situation, the challenges remain significant. We are all indeed under siege, and Migrants wallowing amid Injustice.

CHAPTER TEN

OVERCOMING THE STRUGGLE AS MIGRANTS

Is it possible for a migrant to overcome their challenges and struggles?
Answer: Absolutely. A migrant's experience in their new location will differ significantly from their previous environment. They may encounter various challenges related to language barriers, food differences, cultural adjustments, traditions, and social behaviours.

Explanation for the answer:
Key solutions for addressing the challenges faced by migrants and how they can be resolved include:

- Resolving conflicts.
- Increasing average wealth levels in poor countries.
- Enhancing educational opportunities.
- Improving social security and health insurance systems.
- Combating extreme poverty.
- Addressing discrimination.
- Addressing global warming.
- Minimizing waste production.

Numerous factors can contribute to resolving the challenges faced by migrants. Migration has been a longstanding phenomenon, influenced by economic conditions, natural disasters, socio-political factors, demographic growth, urbanization, conflicts, and family reunification.

Migration Trajectories: Stories of Young Migrants

Migration from Sub-Saharan Africa to the European Union (EU) is one of the most stigmatized forms of migration in the 21st century, heavily shaped by the EU's restrictive migration policies. Consequently, migrants seeking to reach the EU often embark on fragmented and perilous journeys northward.

This contribution seeks to provide deeper empirical insights into these migratory experiences, utilizing a trajectory ethnography approach that combines in-depth interviews with Sub-Saharan Africans currently waiting in Morocco and Turkey to enter the EU. A longitudinal strategy allows for tracking some respondents over extended periods, enabling a better understanding of both anticipated steps and unforeseen developments in their individual migration paths.

By examining three key components—motivation, facilitation, and velocity—this contribution challenges the simplistic, unidirectional metaphors often associated with migration, which suggest that migrants move like flows or waves.

In the past decade, European media have widely circulated images of Sub-Saharan African migrants attempting to reach the EU. These portrayals typically highlight the most dramatic moments of their journeys: the instances when they leap over fences, arrive exhausted in unseaworthy boats on European shores, or conceal themselves in overcrowded cargo trucks. Such representations tend to reinforce public perceptions of African migrants as either desperate invaders or pitiable victims of smuggling networks.

Furthermore, the accompanying narratives often frame this migration from the Global South with an apocalyptic tone, depicting it as an African exodus or invasion. Sub-Saharan African migration to the EU has become one of the most stigmatized forms of human movement in contemporary times.

This contribution aims to enhance the understanding of the journeys undertaken by Sub-Saharan African migrants heading toward the EU. By incorporating the dynamics of their travels before and after the sensational border crossings often highlighted in the media, it strives to present a more comprehensive and nuanced picture of what it means to be on the move in a geopolitical landscape characterized by increasingly closed borders.

African Aspirations and European Borders: Turbulent Migrations to the North

We are living in an era defined by migration. With approximately 214 million international migrants today, migration has reached even the most remote corners of the globe. If individuals do not migrate themselves, they are often intricately connected to those who have crossed state borders. As a cumulative effect, global interconnectedness fuels the desire to relocate, as images of an improved quality of life are easily disseminated worldwide through new media and communication technologies.

Although Africa is frequently perceived as a disconnected continent, from the forces of globalization.

Firstly, Africa maintains connections to the global community through its diasporas, which stay connected with their home communities. Secondly, African societies are increasingly linked through internet access and mobile telephony, with mobile phones reaching areas that have historically lacked landline infrastructure. As a result of both traditional and modern connections, the aspiration to seek better opportunities is pervasive in many African societies.

Migration aspirations often arise during periods when the EU is tightening its borders. From the perspective of European nations, migration from the South is primarily viewed as a security concern. In response, the EU's outer borders have been reinforced, as seen in the Spanish enclaves of Ceuta and Melilla in Morocco. Additional borders are monitored by specialized forces, such as the Rapid Border Intervention Team (RABIT), which was established in Greece in 2010. The digitalization of border controls, including the implementation of transnational databases, is also part of this security framework. Furthermore, EU border controls are increasingly shifting southward, which means that countries of origin for migrants are engaging in lucrative migration agreements that provide them with development aid in exchange for stricter border

regulations and enforcement. For example, between 2007 and 2009, Cape Verde received approximately €27 million from the Spanish government in return for enhanced cooperation in combating irregular migration. Similarly, the European Commission allocated €426 million in development aid to Mali over five years for comparable reasons. Additionally, neighbouring countries of the EU, such as Turkey and Morocco, are increasingly viewed as buffer zones, tasked with managing so-called transit migration.

Due to the EU's restrictive border policies, there have been over 3,700 migration-related fatalities at the EU's borders since the beginning of the 21st century. This stark reality underscores that globalization often results in social closure and restricted access for the most disadvantaged individuals.

The growing interconnectedness of African societies, coupled with the EU's restrictive geopolitical stance on African migration, contributes to a complex and turbulent migration landscape. This turbulence highlights the multifaceted and multidirectional nature of contemporary migration. At the same time, the term "turbulence" reflects the frictions that arise as states and supranational entities strive to control the movement of people. Turbulence serves as a more nuanced alternative to commonly used migration metaphors like "flows" and "waves," which imply unidirectional patterns that may be invasive and encounter minimal resistance.

Fragmented Migration to the North

The rise in migration aspirations during periods of restrictive migration policies in the EU is a significant factor in understanding contemporary irregular migration from Africa to the EU. With many conventional routes blocked, a substantial number of sub-Saharan African migrants embark on fragmented and perilous journeys northward. Several key migration routes can be identified in this context.

First, the Atlantic route from the West African coast to the Canary Islands (part of Spain) has become a favoured path for sub-Saharan Africans seeking to reach the EU. In 2006, over 30,000 sub-Saharan Africans arrived in Spanish territory by boarding fragile boats bound

for the Canaries. A second important route is the trans-Saharan path from West Africa to Morocco, from which migrants aim to make the final leap to Spain, either by entering one of the Spanish enclaves or reaching the Spanish coast by boat. Third, many sub-Saharan African migrants have taken the central Mediterranean route through Libya or Tunisia, aiming for European islands like Malta or Lampedusa (Italy). More recently, sub-Saharan Africans have also begun traveling to Turkey, primarily by airplane, from where they attempt to enter Greece. Typically, migrants reach Greece by boat or by crossing the Greek Turkish land border in the Evros region. However, Turkey serves as a crucial crossroads for migrants from various regions worldwide, meaning that sub-Saharan Africans are only marginally represented in data on irregular migration in this area.

It is important to note that these irregular migration routes from Africa to Europe are not static; they evolve from year to year. The number of arrivals in a given region can be quite high one year and drop significantly the next, potentially rising again in subsequent years.

For instance, the number of irregular arrivals at the Canary Islands fell from over 30,000 in 2006 to 9,600 in 2008 due to stricter sea controls. During the same period, however, the central Mediterranean route to Lampedusa gained prominence, with 21,400 arrivals in 2006 and 31,300 in 2008, only to decline again in 2009, when the number of arrivals in the first six months was at least twice as high as in the same period of 2008. Most irregular migrants in the EU are either visa overstayers or rejected asylum seekers. Therefore, it is not so much an invasion of undocumented individuals that shapes irregular migration to the EU, but rather the limited duration of travel documents and the high number of unsuccessful asylum applications.

While the central Mediterranean route has diminished in significance in recent years, the path from Turkey to Greece has gained traction. The overland route to Greece has been identified by the EU border agency FRONTEX as the last significant gap in the EU's southern border regime, with estimates suggesting that 80% of all irregular migrants to the EU pass through Greece.

In this context, it is crucial to recognize that although the numbers of unauthorized entries may seem substantial, they have a minimal impact on overall immigration statistics to the EU. For example, the 30,000 boat entries at the Canary Islands in 2006 represented only 0.8% of the total non-EU population in Spain that year. Finally, it is worth noting that many irregular migrants in the EU have not crossed the border through unauthorized means.

CHAPTER ELEVEN
UNDERSTANDING MIGRATION TRAJECTORIES

Migration researchers are increasingly focusing on the in-between or mobility phase of migration. Studies examining social networks and smuggling practices have provided valuable insights into how both social and non-social connections facilitate migration processes. While it is possible to identify main routes and entry points, these general patterns offer limited information regarding the dynamics of individual migration journeys.

Additionally, research on transit migration has yielded vital information about migrants in transit as they move toward their destinations. However, this knowledge remains fragmented. Social networks have primarily been studied in isolation from smuggling networks, and most research distinguishes between regular and irregular migration. Although the discourse surrounding transit migration has encouraged scholars to consider the in-between phase more thoroughly, there is still a lack of understanding regarding how this transit phase relates to other stages of the migration process.

This contribution aims to analyse the migration journey in its entirety. It explores how the legal/illegal,

the smuggler/helper, and the mobile/immobile aspects converge within individual migration trajectories.

A Trajectory Ethnography

The findings presented in this study stem from my PhD research (2007–2011), which is framed as a trajectory ethnography. The majority of the data were collected through in-depth interviews with sub-Saharan Africans en route to the EU. Fieldwork began with an exploratory trip to Spain, Morocco, and Senegal, during which initial contacts with migrants and migration-related institutions were established. Following this, I travelled to Morocco (Rabat and Oujda) and Turkey (Istanbul) to gather migration biographies from individuals originating from West and Central African countries. In total, I conducted interviews with 57 migrants in these countries, as well as approximately 50 sub-Saharan Africans residing in the EU regarding their migration journeys.

The interviews conducted with sub-Saharan Africans in Morocco and Turkey were informal and conversational in nature. The research data reflect my interpretation of the migrants' subjective experiences and are not grounded in any form of objectivity. Establishing a trusting relationship with respondents was crucial for gaining a profound understanding of their turbulent trajectories. Consequently, interviews were held in settings where respondents felt comfortable discussing their journeys. Nearly half of the interviews in Morocco and Turkey took place in migrants' homes, while others were conducted in cafés, churches, or outdoor spaces. I intentionally refrained from using recording devices during the interviews. While this off-the-record approach risks losing some relevant data and may affect the credibility of the findings—since the written versions are based on my ad-hoc understanding of the discussions—I believe that the absence of recording technology contributed to a trustworthy environment essential for conducting qualitative research on this often-sensitive topic.

As with any research involving irregular migration, this project entails significant ethical considerations. Specific details about individuals and their strategies could potentially harm them. Therefore, it is imperative for the researcher to clearly communicate the project's objectives to respondents and ensure that participation is entirely voluntary. Additionally, guaranteeing the anonymity of respondents is crucial.

While these steps are essential in the field, I believe researchers can do more without resorting to the naïve notion that the project directly benefits respondents. An open interview approach allows for the inclusion of migrants' agendas within the research project. For instance, researchers can give respondents a voice regarding the topics discussed during interviews and create opportunities for respondents to pose questions to the researcher, facilitating a two-way exchange of information.

In addition to open interviews, I employed a longitudinal strategy throughout this research project. My ethnographic engagement with some respondents enabled me to maintain contact with them after leaving the fieldwork sites in Morocco and Turkey. I followed seven migrants I met in Morocco (three Congolese, two Cameroonians, and two Nigerians) and six migrants I encountered in Turkey (four Nigerians, one Burundian, and one migrant from the Comoros). Unfortunately, all longitudinal respondents were male. Despite interviewing fourteen female migrants in transit spaces within the EU, all attempts to establish long-term connections with them were unsuccessful for various reasons. Nevertheless, these longitudinal cases proved particularly valuable for understanding the trajectories of individual migrants. Through phone conversations and internet chats, I remained updated on their travel experiences. These trans-local connections also allowed me to revisit some migrants in the different countries they settled in, including the Netherlands, France, Italy, and Greece. In these locations, I became part of their daily lives for varying periods. This paper primarily focuses on these longitudinal cases, as they vividly illustrate the complexities of migration trajectories.

Three Main Components of Trajectories

To comprehend the dynamics of migrants' journeys, I conceptualize the primary unit of analysis as the trajectory. Consequently, I do not treat the individual migrant—the actor—as the starting point; rather, I focus on the trajectories themselves, in which migrants' decisions are just one of many factors influencing the journey. Migrants' trajectories are not closed corridors, but rather open, process-oriented phenomena shaped by various influences, including the trajectories of other individuals, objects, capital, regulations, and information. From this relational perspective, the evolution of different trajectories depends on the convergence of multiple factors at specific moments and locations. The researcher's task is to make sense of this convergence to understand the courses of the trajectories.

I identify three main components of journeying:

1. **Motivation for the Journey**: Regardless of whether the move is voluntary or forced, every migrant possesses a motivation to relocate, even if specific goals or destinations have not been articulated. I define this motivation as the migration aspiration, which analytically differs from migrants' intentions, as the former encompasses dreams, wishes, and future perspectives without being directly linked to feasible plans.
2. **Facilitation of the Journey**: While a migrant may be motivated to move, every journey requires facilitation. Some aspects of the journey can be facilitated by the migrant themselves; however, without assistance from others—such as family members, border guards, co-migrants, or even strangers— migrants may struggle to progress. Thus, the facilitation of the journey is rooted in migrants' connections with other individuals.
3. **Velocity of Journeys**: While motivation and facilitation provide direction to journeys, they do not adequately address the pace of travel.

Therefore, the third main component for analysing trajectories is velocity. In this context, migration trajectories encompass not only mobility but also periods of rest, reorientation, and both expected and unexpected temporary or long-term settlements. By considering these factors, I aim to explore the physical and experiential aspects of mobility and immobility to gain deeper insights into the velocity of the trajectories.

In the remainder of this paper, I will elaborate on the dynamics of migrants' trajectories by examining these three components of journeys, focusing on the thirteen longitudinal cases from my study. Each of the following three sections will begin with two snapshots of the trajectories of different migrants, which will then be discussed in relation to the trajectories of other migrants. Thus, while I do not use the migrant as the unit of analysis, I intentionally adopt the perspective of the migrant to better understand their trajectories.

CHAPTER TWELVE

DYNAMIC MOTIVATIONS AND SHIFTING DESTINATIONS

Migrant Narration of Experience

In my country, there is no future. Everyone knows it, and many people leave. They just go! I did the same; I just went! I travelled to Nigeria to seek work. At that time, I did not think of Europe; Nigeria seemed promising, and the economy was booming. So, you go there and search for a place. I had a good life there. But then I heard about

Nigerians leaving for Europe, about their successes, and so on. One day, three of my Nigerian friends devised a plan to go, and I wanted the same. Now, in Morocco, I want to reach Spain. I plan to stay there for one year. After that, I will go to Paris or London, and if the opportunity arises, I will head to New York or Washington!
(Sony, Cameroon, 22 years old. Explaining how his migration to Nigeria influenced his aspiration to reach Europe. Interview in Oujda, Morocco, January 2008)

Of course, I wanted to go to Europe; of course, I dreamed about it. But what can I say? When you

were young, didn't you have your own dreams? That does not mean you can manage it in reality. I know that Europe is not a paradise now; I hear that. So, I can go, but the question is, what can I do? With no papers and no proper education… No, for me, it is better to stay.
(Jean-Louis, Democratic Republic of Congo, 36 years old. Discussing his aspiration to remain in Morocco. Interview in Rabat, Morocco, January 2008)

The two quotes reveal how the aspirations of Sony and Jean-Louis have changed over time. Sony initially went to Nigeria as his first destination, only considering Europe after hearing success stories from Nigerian migrants. In contrast, Jean-Louis explains how his migration project, initially focused on Europe, has evolved into a plan for a longer stay in Morocco.

The fluidity of their aspirations becomes even more intriguing when we note that Jean-Louis did eventually arrive in the EU, while Sony returned to Cameroon. A year after the interview in Rabat, Jean-Louis informed me via email that he felt very discouraged about life in Morocco following a violent incident involving his boss's son. During several telephone conversations, he explained how he managed to borrow a passport from an African migrant living in the UK. With this passport, he was able to take a ferry to Spain, from where he continued on to France. Meanwhile, Sony attempted

several times to cross the Moroccan Spanish border, but all his efforts were in vain. Feeling depressed about his situation in Morocco, he decided to return home to Cameroon. However, as he shared with me during a phone conversation, he has not given up on his aspiration to reach Europe one day. In this sense, a return does not necessarily signify the end of a migration process.

The trajectories of other migrants I have followed exhibit similar dynamics. Due to the dangers and high costs associated with irregular passage to the EU from Morocco and Turkey, several migrants have abandoned their hopes of reaching Europe. Among the thirteen longitudinal cases, one Nigerian migrant in Istanbul chose to return home, while two others (one in Istanbul and one in Rabat)

decided to establish lives in the locations where they initially sought passage.

Like Sony, other respondents explained how the destination of Europe only became apparent to them along the way. One such individual was a Burundian man who received a scholarship to study at a university in Istanbul. His initial plan was to complete his studies in four years and return to Burundi to become a doctor. However, due to the immense workload, language barriers, and daily discrimination in Turkey, he began contemplating an eventual irregular crossing to Greece to build a life in Europe. Another illustrative case is that of a Congolese migrant I met in Morocco. In several conversations, he emphasized his desire to contribute to Moroccan society. He even established a Congolese migrant organization to raise awareness about the presence of African migrants in Morocco.

However, when he was selected by the UNHCR for resettlement, the outcome of his migration project diverged significantly from his aspirations at the time of the interview. Instead of remaining in Morocco, he is now living in the Netherlands due to his resettlement process. These cases highlight the potential for shifting destinations during the migration process.

In addition to these shifting destinations, it is noteworthy that some migrants maintain persistent aspirations of reaching Europe. Several respondents have made multiple life-risking attempts to cross European borders. Literature on transit migration emphasizes that transit migrants in European borderlands often harbour utopian notions of Europe, viewing it as a singular, abstract destination. In other words, Spain and Greece are seen by migrants as access points from which the rest of the EU can be easily reached. Jean-Louis, the Congolese man quoted earlier, travelled overland through Spain to reach France. Two other migrants, from the Comoros and Nigeria, reached Greece after a transit period in Istanbul. From Greece, they subsequently moved to France and Switzerland, respectively. In this context, Europe, as an abstract destination, becomes more concrete along the journey.

While most migration studies focus on the motivations for departure, these findings indicate that motivations may evolve along the way, and migration trajectories do not always unfold according to well-considered plans. As Ralph Grillo suggests, trajectories are often multiple sets of pathways in which destinations shift and may exist in between. In other words, migrants are in motion, but so too are their aspirations.

Moving and Mediating: Migrants' (Dis)Connections

This is a story of a young African:
I started my project without informing my parents.
Only my older brother advised me. We discussed
many things—the difficulties, dangers, and so on. He
also lent me some money to finance the journey.
Then I went to Kano first [a town in northern Nigeria].
I sought traders to transport me to Zinder [a border
town in Niger]. There, I met three other Nigerians. We
became the Nigerian Crew. We were like brothers;
you develop close friendships because you must trust
each other. We ate together, slept together, and
arranged transport together.

*(John, Nigeria, 26 years old. Discussing his overland
journey from Nigeria to Morocco. Interview in Rabat,
Morocco, January 2008)* During a follow-up interview
in Italy, John elaborated on his desert crossing:
People who want to cross to Algeria pass through
Agadez [a migration hub in Niger]. You discuss it with
people in Zinder. In Agadez, we [the Nigerian crew]
had to find a dependable connection man; the border
with Algeria is not easy to cross. It is the desert, you
know! In Morocco, everyone has their own plan, so
we eventually separated. I went with my friend to

Rabat, while the others stayed in Oujda to attempt reaching Europe from there.
(John, Nigeria, 26 years old. Discussing his overland journey from Nigeria to Morocco. Interview in Prato, Italy, November 2008)

You give the contractor the money. This is someone you can trust; in my case, he was a good friend. The contractor must have a reason to stay, so you give him 10% of the price. Once you arrange this, you go to Izmir [a port town south of Istanbul] and take a small boat to Greece. When you reach Greece, you call the contractor to pay the connection man. If you do not reach Greece, you don't pay, and you can try again with the same money.
(Peter, 27 years old. Discussing how migrants arrange their passage from Turkey to Greece. Interview in Istanbul, April 2008) Migrants typically rely on the efforts of others to facilitate their movement. These efforts are necessary not only for organizing the journey in the pre-migration phase but also for coordinating and potentially repairing the journey during transit.

The above accounts illustrate how migrants forge strategic social connections to ensure their passage. John's Nigerian Crew functioned as a collective that supported him in navigating the hazardous crossing of the Sahara Desert. Similarly, the contractor Peter refers to is a social connection that helps prevent economic loss from a failed border crossing. This underscores the notion that migrants often have some negotiating power within the smuggling process. Furthermore, it suggests that

 social networks and smuggling networks are not strictly separate; they may overlap during the migration process.

The theorization of migrants' social networks typically differentiates between strong ties (family members and close friends) and weak ties (connections outside the immediate circle). In other words, the relevant social connections that assist migrants in advancing their journeys are often perceived as solid and durable. However, during my fieldwork in transit spaces, I encountered transient social ties that played a crucial role for migrants during their journeys. In Oujda, a Moroccan town near the Algerian border where many migrants enter Morocco, informal settlements exist where migrants reside for specific periods.

Some attempt to reach Spanish territory from there, while others move to cities like Casablanca or Rabat to find work that helps finance their final leap to the

EU. The communities in these informal settlements are continually refreshed by newcomers who have recently entered Morocco via Algeria. Despite the transient nature of these migrant communities, the social bonds in Oujda are vital, as information about job opportunities and security issues is readily shared.

In Istanbul, I gained valuable insights into social connections in transit situations through my ethnographic engagement with a group of five Nigerians living together in the same house. I visited this house several times, and during these visits, the five friends emphasized their solidarity and friendship. They referred to each other as close brothers. The fact that I met these Nigerians primarily as a collective reinforced my impression of their strong bond. During my stay in Istanbul, I collected their phone numbers and email addresses to maintain contact. This allowed me to observe the outcomes of their so-called transit phase in relation to their friendship. By 2010, two of the five Nigerian friends were still living in Istanbul and maintained regular contact.

Two others had reached Greece, and one of them moved on to Switzerland. One friend returned to Nigeria. Thus, none of the five housemates remained in the same location where I had met them months earlier. The geographical dispersion illustrates the

transient nature of the collective. More interestingly, however, is that most of them became quite distant from each other both geographically and socially. The two men who reached Greece had spent every day together during their time in Istanbul. However, once they were both in Athens, they seldom contacted each other. One of them remarked:
I do not see him very often. He's involved in different businesses and lives in a different area of Athens. Furthermore, when I mentioned to one of the Nigerians still living in Istanbul that his friends had reached Greece, he expressed surprise: Is it? I did not know that. That is good news! I did not know because I was not very engaged with those guys.

What initially was a solid collective at the time of my visit to their Nigerian house turned out to be less cohesive than expected. The transient nature of the group did not imply that the social links between these five young men living together were superficial. Rather, it highlights how social connections can change in the dynamic context of migration trajectories. This issue of temporary attachments is widely recognized in travel literature, as articulated by John J. Leed:
Journeys necessitate the ability both to form attachments and to break them. Travelers, in learning to make contingent, transient, terminable relationships—which are not necessarily superficial— soon become accustomed to forming friendships

quickly, enjoying someone intensely, and then parting with little sorrow. *(quote from J. W. Vogt, 1978)*

The vulnerability of solitary travellers, coupled with their resulting neediness, makes them alert to opportunities for association.

When we analysed social connections during the act of moving, we arrive at a more dynamic understanding of networks that contrasts with the traditional binary of strong and weak ties. Social

connections indeed function as bridges that assist migrants in their migration process. However, it is essential to recognize that these bridges are actively constructed and require ongoing maintenance. Moreover, the case of the Nigerian collective illustrates that these social bridges can sometimes collapse.

Moving and Waiting: The (Im)Mobility of Migrants

You think about moving to Europe, but that is difficult without money. Going back? That is not an option; I cannot go back! If I return, people will ask questions, and some have lent me money; you may understand that. I cannot go back. But that is not the only reason. This football agent [my smuggler] kept my return ticket. So, tell me, how can I afford a ticket to Nigeria? It is impossible! You cannot save money here; you cannot save if you don't have a job. I have been here

for eight months, and if you had told me eight months ago that this would be my life, I would never have left my country.
(Benson, Nigeria, 27 years old. Expressing his frustrations about his immobility in Turkey. Interview in Istanbul, Turkey, April 2008) This country is not easy to navigate; people do not stay here by choice; they are forced to remain. I have been in Oujda for a year now, but sometimes I live in Maghnia [a town on the Algerian side of the border]. I have also spent four days in Rabat.

The situation there is better; you can find housing, there are some jobs, and you have a nice bed to sleep in. But there's one thing I dislike about that place: people forget where they are going. They forget about Europe; they lose sight of their dreams and their spirit. I prefer to stay here [in Oujda] because every day when I wake up, I realize that I must go. Look around you; this is not a place to stay. *(Sona, Cameroon, 22 years old. Discussing his mobile (im)life in Morocco. Interview in Oujda, Morocco, January 2008)* As the preceding accounts illustrate, one cannot focus solely on the moving aspects to understand the dynamics of migrant trajectories.

The migration processes of sub-Saharan Africans passing through Morocco and Turkey are highly fragmented and include significant periods of immobility. In terms of migrants' immobile status, three groups can be distinguished. First, there are stranded migrants who feel that EU borders have blocked their movement northward. Sona, the Cameroonian man, exemplifies this group. Secondly, there are stuck migrants who experience a form of immobility in every direction, including return to their countries of origin. Jude represents a stuck migrant, as he is unable to move onward to the EU and cannot return to Nigeria either. Finally, there are settled migrants—those who are content to remain in a transit country.

It has already been established that migrants' aspirations are fluid. In line with this, migrants should not be viewed as fixed within one of the three categories of immobility. A sense of home may deteriorate, prompting a migrant to decide to move again. Conversely, a transit situation may evolve into a home-like experience for the individual in question. This is illustrated by Sona, who compares the situation in Oujda, where migrants wait without interacting with Moroccan society, to Rabat, where African migrants gradually become more settled. In Sona's words, Rabat is a place where people forget they are on their way to the EU.

In this regard, it is important to distinguish between experienced immobility and physical immobility. Migrants who claim to be immobile may be moving over short or long distances. Many migrants stated they are on the move for security and economic reasons. Some respondents in Rabat emphasized that they avoid begging in the same places to prevent issues with the local population and authorities. In Istanbul, many sub-Saharan Africans engage in instant and mobile economic activities known as *chabuk chabuk*, meaning "do it quickly" or "hurry up." These fleeting activities, such as carrying heavy loads in markets and construction sites, are difficult for authorities to monitor and are therefore reserved for migrants without legal status.

While Jude's account points to an inability to cross international borders, Sona can move frequently across the Moroccan Algerian border. Thus, migrants who appear immobile may, in fact, cross international borders. Some Nigerian and Senegalese migrants in Istanbul shared their strategy of commuting between their countries of origin and the transit country to reach the EU. Before their visa for Turkey expires (usually after three months), they return to their home countries, knowing that a proper return increases the likelihood of a successful visa application for the same country. With a new visa, they may attempt to reach the EU again. In these instances, the transit phase takes on a circular and mobile character.

Migrants who successfully reach Europe after a period of immobility in the European borderlands often face another waiting period in Europe, specifically in detention. In nearly all southern European countries, authorities have recently extended the maximum detention periods for irregular migrants. In Greece, the maximum detention period is six months, and in exceptional cases, twelve months. In Italy, the maximum period is set at 180 days. In Spain, it remains at forty days, while Malta is an extreme case, with a maximum detention duration of eighteen months, the highest limit allowed under EU rules.

When authorities cannot identify the transit point or country of origin of a detained migrant, the individual is typically released with an expulsion order, requiring them to leave the country within a specified period. This period often prompts many migrants to become mobile once again. It is interesting to note where the longitudinal respondents have ended up. Only six of the thirteen migrants I have followed have reached the EU. Here is an overview:

- Clement (48 years old, Democratic Republic of Congo) moved from Morocco to France by airplane and recently applied for asylum there.
- Jean (36 years old, Democratic Republic of Congo) travelled from Morocco to Spain by boat using a borrowed passport. He later moved north to France, where he applied for asylum.

- John (26 years old, Nigeria) journeyed from Morocco through Algeria and Libya, reaching Italy. He now resides in Prato, where he has a girlfriend (from Nigeria but holding an Italian passport) who recently gave birth to their child. His new role as a father enhances his chances for regularization in Italy.
- Destiny (31 years old, Nigeria) reached Greece by boarding a fragile boat from Turkey. Unhappy in Greece, he moved to Italy, later heading to Switzerland, where he applied for asylum. However, Swiss authorities rejected his application. Consequently, Destiny decided to return to Italy, where he is formulating new plans.
- Joseph (27 years old, Nigeria) reached Greece by boarding a fragile boat to a Greek island. He currently commutes between Athens and the tourist island of Corfu, where he participates in informal tourism services.
- Said (42 years old, Comoros) also reached Greece by boat. He applied for asylum, pretending to be from Somalia, and his application was accepted. With his asylum papers, he flew to France, where he now lives as an irregular migrant in Marseille (having discarded his asylum papers).

Interestingly, only John and Benson remained in the European countries they initially entered. The other four migrants crossed.

CHAPTER THIRTEEN
TWO MEANINGS OF TRAJECTORY

Migration is frequently perceived as a straightforward transition from an origin to a destination. In migration studies, migrants are often depicted as rational actors who make decisions in place A regarding how to reach their destination, place B. Consequently, the journey is often trivialized as a mere in-between phase. I have challenged this linear perspective of migration by examining the experiences of a specific group: sub-Saharan Africans who aspire to reach the EU but lack the necessary travel documents. For these individuals, the journey to the EU is highly fragmented, with border crossings rarely occurring without complications. Their trajectories exhibit a process-oriented logic, where destinations are fluid, social connections can be ephemeral, and periods of mobility can easily shift to periods of immobility, and vice versa.

Adopting this dynamic perspective allows us to critically assess the public discourse surrounding irregular migration, as outlined at the beginning of this article. This discourse portrays irregular migration from Africa to Europe as a phenomenon characterized by waves of migrants inundating European territories. Often, this is illustrated through migration maps that depict large arrows simply connecting one continent to another. Many of these maps fail to capture the multi-directionality,

fragmentation, and processes that define the trajectories I have studied.

To analytically grasp the dynamics of these trajectories, I propose that we must consider two interpretations of the term "trajectory." First, there is the anthropological understanding of a trajectory as a life or career path, which suggests that individuals have varying aspirations and make different decisions at different life stages. This implies that similar events hold different significance for migrants depending on when they occur in their life journeys. Second, there is the geographical trajectory, which denotes movement across space. While I do not advocate for geographical determinism, I contend that the spatial evolution of a trajectory influences its continuation. Being in one location may evoke a desire to reach another, and once one arrives at that destination, new aspirations may arise—or the desire to return to the previous location may resurface.

Following this reasoning, it is not merely the beginnings (point A) and endings (point B) that are significant, but rather the journey itself—the trajectory in between.

CHAPTER FOURTEEN

BIGGEST CHALLENGE FACING MIGRANTS

Here are the eight most significant challenges facing migrants today—and what you can do to tackle them.

1. **Language Barriers**
   Language barriers present a primary challenge for migrants, as they significantly hinder effective communication. It is often assumed that immigrants will learn English or French, depending on their preferences. This assumption can adversely affect their ability to make informed decisions and negatively impact their overall care experience. Additionally, language barriers can exacerbate other forms of disadvantage. In some countries, immigrants receive substandard healthcare due to their limited proficiency in the native language. Furthermore, differences between the languages spoken by first-generation and second-generation migrants can create additional challenges.

2. **Lack of Employment Opportunities**
   Immigrants frequently encounter discrimination in the job market, stemming from systemic

issues related to job design and management. Many immigrant workers are excluded from labour and safety protections that are available to native-born employees. Newly arrived immigrants often lack knowledge of the local job

market, while immigrant professionals struggle to have their foreign academic credentials

recognized. To address these challenges, improved policies are essential to help reduce the barriers that refugees face in securing employment.

3. **Housing**

Immigrants are among the most vulnerable populations when it comes to housing. They face significant challenges in finding safe, decent, and affordable accommodations. The issues surrounding housing for immigrants extend beyond homeownership rates; many recently settled immigrants are unemployed and unable to afford rent. Additionally, undocumented immigrants often bear a greater housing cost burden compared to their legal counterparts. These housing challenges necessitate coordinated national and local responses. Those who manage to secure better housing should consider implementing robust security measures, such as Identity Theft Protection, to safeguard their personal information.

4. **Access to Medical Services**
   Access to healthcare services should be a fundamental right for all individuals, regardless of their nationality. However, immigrants often experience low rates of medical insurance

   coverage and limited access to healthcare services. Policy changes have further restricted.

immigrants' access to insurance and healthcare, leading to barriers that include financial constraints, discrimination, and fear of deportation. These factors have raised concerns about immigrants' ability to participate in free healthcare programs. In many countries, undocumented immigrants are ineligible for health insurance, and research indicates that immigrant families frequently forgo necessary medical care due to fears of discrimination. Additionally, many immigrants do not qualify for subsidized participation in national health insurance programs.

5. **Transportation Issues**
   Reliable transportation is crucial for completing everyday tasks, yet immigrants often face limited options. One significant challenge is the age-related unreliability of their vehicles, which can hinder their ability to commute to work. Many immigrants encounter auto-related issues, including difficulties obtaining a driver's license, further complicating their transportation situation.
6. **Cultural Differences**
   Misunderstandings and myths about immigrants can lead to significant cultural barriers. Even well-settled migrants may continue to

   experience cultural and communication challenges, ranging from social customs to

more profound issues such as religion. For example, children may feel embarrassed if they are unfamiliar with popular music. Fear and distrust of immigrants have perpetuated cultural myths in many societies, and even well-intentioned actions can sometimes be perceived as culturally insensitive. It is essential for individuals to maintain an open mind and refrain from viewing differences as negative.

7. **Raising Children**

   Children of immigrant parents face unique challenges as they grow up in a new country. Socioeconomic and psychosocial issues can create significant hurdles, leading to increased rates of depression, anxiety, and panic disorders among these children. The pressure they experience is often compounded by a lack of mental health support. Unlike adults, children are still in the process of forming their identities, and navigating between two cultures can lead to internal conflicts. Research indicates that children of immigrants are more likely to struggle academically and may face discrimination, isolation, and financial stress.

8. **Prejudice**

   Many immigrants endure discrimination, and there has been a notable rise in anti-

   immigration sentiment. Such prejudices are often fuelled by the media and the information individuals consume, which can reinforce restrictive policies. Discrimination tends to target various minority ethnic and religious groups, with non-EU migrants in the UK reporting higher levels of perceived

discrimination compared to their European counterparts. In response, many governments are intensifying efforts to combat discrimination and promote integration, leading to an increase in anti-racism and prejudice reduction campaigns in the media.

Final Thoughts

One billion people—one-seventh of the world's population—are migrants. Despite the challenges they face, immigrants will continue to play a vital role in every community and economy.

CHAPTER FIFTEEN

ECONOMY AND SOCIAL IMPACT OF
MIGRANT

Is Migration Beneficial for the Economy?

Migration is a significant aspect of social and economic life in many countries, but the characteristics of migrant populations can vary widely. This variation is influenced by the diverse sources of migration. For instance, in much of Europe, citizens enjoy extensive rights to free movement, while in countries like Australia, Canada, and New Zealand, managed labour migration plays a crucial role. Other sources of migration include family reunification and humanitarian efforts. Regardless of its origin, migration has profound effects on our societies, often sparking controversy. The economic impact of migration is no exception.

Benefit or Burden — What is the Reality?

To address this question, it is useful to examine migration's effects in three key areas: the labour market, the public purse, and economic growth.

Labor Markets

- Over the past decade, migrants accounted for 47% of the increase in the workforce in the United States and 70% in Europe.
- Migrants occupy essential roles in both fast-growing and declining sectors of the economy.
- Similar to native-born individuals, young migrants tend to be better educated than those nearing retirement.
- Migrants significantly enhance labour market flexibility, particularly in Europe.

The Public Purse

- Migrants contribute more in taxes and social contributions than they receive in benefits.
- Labor migrants have the most positive impact on the public purse.
- Employment is the primary determinant of migrants' net fiscal contribution.

Economic Growth

- Migration increases the working-age population.
- Migrants arrive with valuable skills and contribute to the human capital development of host countries.
- They also play a role in technological advancement. Understanding these impacts is

  crucial for societies to engage in meaningful discussions about the role of migration.

Such discussions are essential for formulating policies in areas like education and employment that maximize the benefits of migration, particularly by

 improving migrants' employment outcomes. This policy framework will naturally differ from country to country. However, the fundamental question of how to optimize the benefits of migration for both host countries and migrants themselves must be addressed by many OECD nations in the coming decades, especially as rapid population aging increases the demand for migrants to fill workforce gaps.

Migrant workers make significant contributions to the labour market across both high- and low-skilled occupations. In the last ten years, immigrants accounted for 47% of the increase in the workforce in the United States and 70% in Europe (OECD, 2012). In OECD countries, only a small portion of these workforce entrants came through managed labour migration, while a larger share arrived through family, humanitarian, and free-movement channels. Notably, immigrants represented about a quarter of entries into

the most rapidly declining occupations in Europe (24%) and the United States (28%). In Europe, these declining occupations include craft and related trades, as well as machine operators and assemblers; in the United States, they primarily involve production, installation, maintenance, and repair jobs. In these sectors, immigrants are fulfilling labour demands by taking on positions that domestic workers often view as unattractive or lacking in career prospects.

In Europe, free movement migration helps mitigate labour market imbalances. The scope of labour mobility significantly increased within the EU/EFTA zones following the EU enlargements of 2004 and 2007, enhancing labour market adjustment capacity.

Recent estimates suggest that migration may have absorbed as much as a quarter of the asymmetric labour market shock occurring at different times and intensities across countries (Jauer et al., 2014).

Migrants contribute more to taxes and social contributions than they receive in individual benefits. Recent research on the fiscal impact of migration in European OECD countries, as well as Australia, Canada, and the United States, has provided new and internationally comparative evidence (Liebig and Mo, 2013). This study indicates that the cumulative waves of migration over the past 50 years in OECD countries have had an average impact close to zero, rarely exceeding 0.5% of GDP in either positive or

negative terms. The impact is most pronounced in Switzerland and Luxembourg, where immigrants provide an estimated net benefit of about 2% of GDP to the public purse. Therefore, immigrants are neither a burden on the public purse nor a cure-all for fiscal challenges. In most countries, except those with a significant share of older migrants, immigrants contribute more to taxes and social contributions than they receive in benefits. This means they aid in financing public infrastructure, albeit to a lesser extent than native-born individuals. Contrary to widespread belief, low-educated immigrants often have a better fiscal position—reflected in the difference between their contributions and the benefits they receive—than their native-born counterparts. In cases where immigrants have a less favourable fiscal position, it is not due to a greater reliance on social benefits but rather because they typically earn lower wages and consequently contribute less.

The fiscal gains in many European OECD countries, such as Belgium, France, and Sweden, could result in a budget impact exceeding 0.5% of GDP. This would also assist immigrants in achieving their own goals: most immigrants do not come seeking social benefits but rather to find work and improve their lives and those of their families. Therefore, efforts to better integrate immigrants should be viewed as an investment rather than a cost.

Cross-Country Migration and Economic Growth
International migration has both direct and indirect effects on economic growth. It is widely acknowledged that expanding the workforce through migration can lead to an increase in aggregate GDP. However, the situation is less clear regarding per capita GDP growth.

The differences in the fiscal positions of immigrant households are influenced by the design of tax and

benefit systems and, more significantly, by variations in the composition of the migrant population concerning age and entry category. In countries where recent labour migrants constitute a substantial portion of the immigrant population, their fiscal position tends to be much more favourable than in countries where humanitarian migrants make up a significant share. While labour migrants generally have a more positive impact than other migrant groups, there is a trend toward convergence over time. Conversely, the fiscal position of immigrants is typically less favourable in countries with longstanding immigrant populations and limited recent labour immigration. Employment is the most critical factor determining migrants' net fiscal contribution, especially in countries with generous welfare states. Raising the employment rate of immigrants to match that of native-born individuals would significantly alter the age structure of receiving

countries. Migrants tend to be concentrated in younger, economically active age groups compared to natives, thereby helping to reduce dependency ratios (Gagnon, 2014).

Furthermore, migrants arrive with skills and abilities that complement the human capital of the host country. Evidence from the United States indicates that skilled immigrants contribute to enhancing research, innovation, and technological progress (Hunt, 2010). The proportion of highly educated

immigrants in OECD countries is rapidly increasing. The number of tertiary-educated immigrants in OECD countries surged by 70% over the past decade, reaching nearly 30 million by 2010/11. Of these, approximately 5 million, or 17%, arrived in the last five years, primarily driven by migration from Asia, which accounted for more than 2 million tertiary-educated migrants in the past five years (OECD-UNDESA, 2013).

Despite this, few empirical studies have attempted to estimate the overall impact of net migration on economic growth, partly due to a lack of harmonized comparative data on international migration by skill levels. One study examining the impact of migration on economic growth across 22 OECD countries from 1986 to 2006 found a positive but modest effect of the human capital brought by migrants on economic

growth. The contribution of immigrants to human capital accumulation tends to counteract the mechanical dilution effect (i.e., the impact of population increases on capital per worker), yet the net effect remains small, even in countries with highly selective migration policies. An increase of 50% in net migration of the foreign-born results in less than a one-tenth of a percentage point variation in productivity growth (Boubtane and Dumont, 2013).

The educational status of immigrants varies significantly. Like the relationship between younger

and older native-born individuals, young immigrants are generally more educated than those nearing retirement. This trend holds true for immigrants entering the labour force: on average, over a third are tertiary educated, while the same proportion has not completed their upper secondary education. Since 2000/01, immigrants have accounted for 31% of the increase in the highly educated labour force in Canada, 21% in the United States, and 14% in Europe.

Although most migration is not directly driven by workforce needs, immigrants play a vital role in the most dynamic sectors of the economy. New immigrants represented 22% of entries into rapidly growing occupations in the United States and 15% in

Europe, notably in healthcare and STEM (Science, Technology, Engineering, and Mathematics) fields.

The substantial contributions of migrants to the social and economic fabric of developed nations cannot be overstated. Individuals from all walks of life and backgrounds deserve respect and recognition for their contributions.

Unfortunately, migrants continue to face challenges and discrimination from their host nations, and this must end.

CHAPTER SIXTEEN

COMPARE AND CONTRAST THE ADVANTAGES AND DISAVANTAGES OF MIGRANTS

Migration: Advantages and Disadvantages

Migration refers to the movement of individuals or their belongings from one location to another, often across significant distances. Proponents of immigration argue that it enhances the economy by expanding the labour force and fostering innovation. Conversely, opponents contend that immigration negatively impacts low-skilled native workers by occupying jobs that citizens might otherwise secure or by suppressing wages for those workers.

Benefits and Challenges of Migration:

Migration can offer numerous advantages, such as providing refuge from war, natural disasters, or economic difficulties. However, it also presents challenges, including the displacement of local communities and the potential erosion of cultural identities. For instance, many individuals have migrated to the United States over recent decades, often settling in new cities or communities. While some view migration as a pathway to greater opportunities, it is essential to recognize the complexities involved.

Students can explore additional advantages and disadvantages of migration through various articles on topics like events, individuals, sports, and technology. Nevertheless, significant challenges persist, with one of the most notable being the language barrier. Individuals who lack proficiency in English may find it difficult to secure employment in the United States. Moreover, the migration process can be arduous and stressful. However, careful planning can

facilitate a smoother transition with minimal stress. This article will delve into the advantages and disadvantages of migration, along with tips to ensure a successful experience.

Advantages of Migration:

- Developing countries benefit from remittances.
- Reduction of unemployment.
- Job vacancies can be filled.
- Economic growth is stimulated.
- Areas with aging populations can receive rejuvenation.

- Additional tax revenue for the host country.
- Introduction of new innovations and ideas.

Disadvantages of Migration:

- Loss of financial and informational wealth.
- Drain of skilled labour.
- Wage suppression.
- Potential neglect of employee benefit programs by companies.
- Risk of exploitation and increased crime rates.
- Strain on public services.
- Job displacement.
- Time required for migrants to adapt to new environments.

Advantages of Migration for Host Countries:

Migration can yield several benefits for host countries, including:

- **Filling Job Vacancies:** Migration can address skill gaps within the workforce, enhance business productivity, and contribute to national economic growth.
- **Economic Growth:** The economic advantages of low-skilled labour migration often surpass the associated risks and costs.

Immigrants can be integral to the cultural and economic fabric of many nations.

- **Support for Aging Populations:** As economies stagnate and fewer young people settle in certain areas, migrants can invigorate local economies with their skills and ideas.
- **Increased Tax Revenue:** In the face of demographic challenges, accepting immigrants can help fill the pension gap and contribute to tax revenues.
- **New Ideas and Innovations:** Research indicates that immigrants positively impact society by contributing to economic growth and filling skill gaps within the native population.

Disadvantages of Migration for Host Countries:

However, migration also brings challenges, such as:

- **Wage Depression:** Increased competition for jobs can lead to lower wages, as some migrants may accept lower-paying positions to maintain their living standards.
- **Neglect of Employee Benefits:** The influx of migrant workers can result in companies cutting costs by offering lower wages and fewer benefits, leading to decreased worker productivity.
- **Exploitation Risks:** Migrants may face exploitation due to language barriers or reliance on individuals who may not have their best interests at heart.

- **Strain on Public Services:** A growing population can overwhelm public services, necessitating the construction of new infrastructure, schools, and healthcare facilities.

-

- **Job Displacement:** High levels of immigration can lead to job displacement and increased unemployment, along with heightened crime rates and health risks.

  Adaptation Challenges: Migrants often face difficulties integrating into their new environments, including language barriers and potential discrimination.

- **Increased Crime Rates:** The ease of movement associated with migration can facilitate organized crime and human trafficking.

Advantages of Migration for Countries of Origin:

There are also benefits for countries of origin, including:

- **Remittances:** Migrants frequently send money back home, bolstering the economies of developing countries and supporting investments in infrastructure, healthcare, and education.

- **Unemployment Reduction:** Migration can enhance economic stability and productivity in the home country.
- **Skill Development:** Returning migrants often bring back valuable skills, contacts, and resources that can drive economic growth and innovation.

Disadvantages of Migration for Countries of Origin:

However, migration can also have negative effects on countries of origin:

- **Loss of Financial and Informational Wealth:** High levels of migration can result in a significant reduction in economic contributions from the younger population.
- **Loss of Skilled Labor:** The emigration of qualified professionals, such as doctors, can create shortages in essential services.
-
- **Negative Impact on Children:** Families left behind may struggle, leading to social issues such as orphanhood and vulnerability among children.

Conclusion:

Migration can be a beneficial option for many individuals, but it is crucial to weigh the pros and cons before making such a crucial decision. Beyond economic motivations, personal values and political circumstances often drive the desire to migrate. Migration is a multifaceted issue that requires a nuanced understanding of its advantages and disadvantages, as well as the individual motivations behind it.

FAQs on Migration:

Question 1: What is Migration?
Answer: Migration is a natural part of life, as individuals seek new opportunities and environments. The phrase "the grass is greener on the other side" reflects the belief that other places may offer better circumstances. Often, this belief proves true as people relocate in search of improved jobs, education, and social support.

Question 2: What are the advantages and disadvantages of Migration?
Answer: Migration involves moving from one country to another or within regions of the same country. Advantages include enhanced economic opportunities, cultural enrichment, and reduced environmental impact. Conversely, disadvantages may involve exploitation risks, loss of cultural identity, and limited access to essential resources like healthcare and education.

Question 3: Is migration a good thing?
Answer: Migration can be advantageous, but it also presents challenges. It enables individuals to travel, forge new friendships, and improve their quality of life. However, migrants often face prejudice and discrimination based on their backgrounds, beliefs, or origins.

CHAPTER SEVENTEEN
HEROS PAST

This page is dedicated to honouring our past heroes.

While there are many heroes in today's world, it is essential to acknowledge the sacrifices made by those who came before us. Failing to recognize their contributions would be an injustice to the ultimate sacrifices they made for Africans to reach our current standing as a people.

Dr. Martin Luther King Jr. (January 15, 1929 – April 14, 1968) was an American Christian minister and activist who became the most prominent spokesperson and leader of the civil rights movement in the United States.

Malcolm X (May 19, 1925 – February 21, 1965) was an African American Muslim minister and human rights activist, widely recognized as a significant figure during the civil rights movement.

Nelson Mandela (July 18, 1918 – December 5, 2013) was a South African anti-apartheid revolutionary, political leader, and philanthropist who served as the President of South Africa from 1994 to 1999. He was the country's first black head of state and the first elected in a fully representative democratic election.

Dr. Kwame Nkrumah (September 21, 1909 – April 27, 1972) was a Ghanaian politician, political theorist, and revolutionary. He was the first Prime Minister and President of Ghana, leading the Gold Coast to independence from Britain in 1957 and advocating for the independence of all African nations.

Kenneth David Kaunda (April 28, 1924 – June 17, 2021), known as KK, was a Zambian politician who served as the first President of Zambia from 1964 to 1991. He played a crucial role in the struggle for independence from British rule.

Jomo Kenyatta (1897 – 1978) was a Kenyan anti-colonial activist and politician who governed Kenya as its Prime Minister from 1963 to 1964 and then as its first President from 1964 until his death in 1978.

Julius Nyerere, born in Butiama, Mara (then part of the British colony of Tanganyika), was the son of a Zanaki chief. After completing his education, he studied at Makerere College in Uganda and then at Edinburgh University in Scotland. In 1952, he returned to Tanganyika, married, and worked as a schoolteacher.

Marcus Garvey (August 17, 1887 – June 10, 1940) was a Jamaican political activist, Black nationalist, publisher, journalist, entrepreneur, and orator.

Rosa Parks (February 4, 1913 – October 24, 2005) was an American activist in the civil rights movement, best known for her pivotal role in the Montgomery bus boycott.

Bob Marley (February 6, 1945 – May 11, 1981) was a Jamaican singer, songwriter, and musician. Regarded as one of the pioneers of reggae, his musical career blended elements of reggae, ska, and rocksteady, along with his distinctive vocal and songwriting style. Marley's contributions to music elevated the visibility of Jamaican music globally and established him as a significant figure in popular culture for over a decade.

Mary Seacole (November 3, 1805 – May 14, 1881) was a British Jamaican businesswoman who established the British Hotel behind the lines during the Crimean War.

Ahmadu Ibrahim Bello (June 12, 1910 – January 15, 1966), knighted as Sir Ahmadu Bello, was a conservative Nigerian statesman who played a pivotal role in guiding Northern Nigeria through its independence in 1960. He served as its first and only premier from 1954 until his assassination in 1966.

Muhammad Ali (January 17, 1942 – June 3, 2016) was an American professional boxer, activist, and philanthropist. Known as "The Greatest," he is widely regarded as one of the most significant and celebrated figures of the 20th century and one of the greatest boxers of all time.

Harriet Tubman (March 1822 – March 10, 1913) was an American abolitionist and political activist. Born into slavery, she escaped and subsequently made approximately 13 missions to rescue around 70 enslaved people, including family and friends, using the network of anti-slavery activists and safe houses known as the Underground Railroad.

Chief Obafemi Awolowo (March 6, 1909) was the first Leader of Government Business and Minister of Local Government and Finance, and the first Premier of the Western Region under Nigeria's parliamentary system, serving from 1952 to 1959. He was the official

Leader of the Opposition in the federal parliament to the Balewa government from 1959 to 1963.

Many men and women have contributed to the progress of our cities and nations, shaping the foundation of the entire Black race. We must build upon their legacy so that future generations of Africans will be proud of our shared history.

Mary Seacole. Born 3rd November 1805 - Died 14th May 1881 (aged 75), Mary was a British Jamaican businesswoman who set up the British Hotel behind the lines during the Crimean War.

Rosa Parks. Born 4th February 1913 - Died 24th October 2005 (aged 92), Rosa was an American activist in the civil rights movement best known for her pivotal role in the Montgomery bus boycott.

Nelson Mandela, a prominent figure in the struggle against apartheid and a symbol of peace and reconciliation, was born on July 18, 1918. His remarkable life journey came to an end on December 5, 2013. Throughout his 95 years, Mandela dedicated himself to the fight for justice and equality, becoming the first black president of South Africa and a global icon for human rights. His legacy continues to inspire generations around the world.

Muhammad Ali, born on January 17, 1942, and passing away on June 3, 2016, at the age of 74, was an iconic American professional boxer, renowned activist, and dedicated philanthropist. Often referred to by his celebrated nickname, "The Greatest," Ali is widely recognized as one of the most influential and revered figures of the 20th century. His remarkable career in boxing not only earned him numerous accolades, including three-time world heavyweight champion titles, but also established him as a cultural icon whose impact extended far beyond the ring.

Ali's charisma, eloquence, and unwavering commitment to social justice made him a prominent voice during a time of significant social upheaval in the United States. He was an outspoken advocate for civil rights and religious freedom, famously refusing to be drafted into the Vietnam War on the grounds of his religious beliefs and opposition to the conflict, which resulted in a landmark Supreme Court case. His legacy is further enriched by his philanthropic efforts, which included initiatives aimed at promoting peace, education, and health care for underserved communities.

In addition to his athletic prowess, Ali's ability to inspire and connect with people from all walks of life solidified his status as a global ambassador for humanitarian causes. His life story is a testament to the power of resilience, conviction, and the pursuit of excellence, making him not only one of the greatest boxers of all time but also a lasting source of inspiration for generations to come.

Dr. Kwame Nkrumah, born on September 21, 1909, and passing on April 27, 1972, was a prominent Ghanaian politician, influential political theorist, and revolutionary leader whose impact on the African continent is still felt today. He served as the first Prime Minister and later as the President of Ghana, playing a pivotal role in the country's journey to independence from British colonial rule in 1957. Nkrumah's vision for a united Africa and his advocacy for Pan-Africanism were instrumental in shaping the political landscape of the region. His leadership not only marked a significant turning point for Ghana but also inspired numerous independence movements across Africa, as he championed the ideals of self-governance, social justice, and economic empowerment. Throughout his life, Nkrumah remained a fervent advocate for the rights of the African people, and his legacy continues to influence contemporary discussions on governance and development in the post-colonial context.

132

Kenneth David Kaunda, GCIH SCOT (28 April 1924 -
17 June 2021), widely recognized by his initials KK,
was a prominent Zambian politician and a pivotal
figure in the nation's history. He served as the
inaugural President of Zambia from 1964 until 1991, a
period marked by significant political and social
transformation. Kaunda was not only a key leader in
the Zambian struggle for independence from British
colonial rule, but he also played an instrumental role
in the broader movement for decolonization across
Africa. His vision for a united and independent
Zambia was characterized by his commitment to
social justice, education, and healthcare. Throughout
his presidency, Kaunda implemented various policies
aimed at fostering national unity and economic
development, although his tenure was also marked
by challenges, including economic difficulties and
political dissent. His legacy continues to influence
Zambian politics and society, as he is remembered
for his contributions to the country's independence
and his efforts to promote Pan-Africanism.

Jomo Kenyatta, born around 1897 and passing away on August 22, 1978, was a significant figure in Kenya's struggle for independence and played a crucial role in shaping the nation's political landscape. As a prominent anti-colonial activist, he dedicated much of his life to advocating for the rights and freedoms of the Kenyan people against British colonial rule. His leadership and vision were instrumental in mobilizing support for the independence movement.

Kenyatta first served as the Prime Minister of Kenya from 1963 to 1964, during which time he laid the groundwork for the newly independent nation and addressed various socio-economic challenges. Following this pivotal role, he became Kenya's first President in 1964, a position he held until his death in 1978. Under his presidency, Kenyatta focused on nation-building, promoting unity among the diverse ethnic groups within Kenya, and implementing policies aimed at economic development. His legacy is marked by both his contributions to the fight for independence and the complex political landscape that emerged during his administration.

Marcus Garvey, born on August 17, 1887, in St. Ann's Bay, Jamaica, and who departed this life on June 10, 1940, at the age of fifty-two, was a prominent Jamaican political activist whose influence extended far beyond his homeland. A fervent advocate of black nationalism, Garvey dedicated his life to the empowerment and upliftment of people of African descent around the globe. He was not only a passionate orator but also a prolific publisher and journalist, utilizing his writing to spread his vision of racial pride and self-reliance. As an entrepreneur, he founded the Universal Negro Improvement Association (UNIA), which aimed to unite and promote the interests of black people worldwide. His legacy as a leader and visionary continues to resonate, inspiring generations in the ongoing struggle for civil rights and social justice.

Malcolm X, born on May 19, 1925, in Omaha, Nebraska, and tragically passing away on February 21, 1965, at the age of thirty-nine, was a profoundly influential African American Muslim minister, activist, and a pivotal figure in the struggle for human rights. His life journey was marked by significant transformation, as he evolved from a troubled youth into a powerful orator and advocate for the rights of African Americans. Throughout the civil rights movement, he emerged as a prominent voice, challenging systemic racism and advocating for black empowerment and self-determination. His eloquent speeches and writings resonated deeply with many, inspiring a generation to confront social injustices and fight for equality. Malcolm X's legacy continues to influence contemporary discussions on race, identity, and justice in America.

Maya Angelou, born on April 4, 1928, and passing away on May 28, 2014, at the age of 86, was a distinguished American poet, memoirist, and civil rights activist whose influence extended far beyond the realm of literature. Throughout her prolific career, she authored seven autobiographies that eloquently chronicled her life experiences, as well as three insightful books of essays that explored themes of identity, resilience, and social justice. In addition to her autobiographical works, Angelou published several celebrated volumes of poetry, which resonated deeply with readers and often addressed the complexities of the human experience.

Her contributions to the arts and culture are further highlighted by her involvement in a wide array of plays, films, and television shows, showcasing her versatility and talent across different mediums. Over the course of more than five decades, Angelou's work not only enriched the literary landscape but also played a pivotal role in the civil rights movement, where she used her voice to advocate for equality and justice. Her legacy continues to inspire and empower individuals around the world, making her an enduring figure in American history and literature.

Bob Marley, born on February 6, 1945, in Nine Mile, Jamaica, and who sadly passed away on May 11, 1981, at the age of thirty-six, was an iconic Jamaican singer, songwriter, and musician whose influence on the music world remains profound. Widely celebrated as one of the pioneering figures of reggae music, Marley's artistic journey was marked by a remarkable fusion of various musical genres, including reggae, ska, and rocksteady. His distinctive vocal style, characterized by its emotive delivery and rich timbre, coupled with his profound songwriting abilities, allowed him to craft songs that resonated deeply with audiences across the globe.

Throughout his career, Marley produced a series of groundbreaking albums that not only showcased his musical versatility but also addressed themes of social justice, love, and resistance. His lyrics often reflected the struggles and aspirations of the marginalized, making his music a powerful vehicle for social change. Songs like "No Woman, No Cry," "One Love," and "Redemption Song" have become anthems that transcend cultural and geographical boundaries, solidifying his status as a global icon.

Marley's contributions to music significantly enhanced the global visibility of Jamaican music, paving the way for future generations of artists. His ability to blend traditional Jamaican sounds with international influences helped to popularize reggae on a worldwide scale, establishing him as a prominent figure in popular culture for over a decade. Even after his untimely death, Bob Marley's legacy continues to inspire musicians and fans alike, ensuring that his message of unity, peace, and resilience endures through the ages.

Harriet Tubman, who was born in March 1822 and passed away in 1913 at the remarkable age of 90, stands out as a pivotal figure in American history, renowned for her tireless efforts as an abolitionist and political activist. Born into the harsh realities of slavery in Maryland, Tubman faced unimaginable challenges from a young age. However, her indomitable spirit led her to escape from bondage, an act of bravery that marked the beginning of her lifelong commitment to the fight for freedom.

Following her own escape, Tubman became a key conductor on the Underground Railroad, a clandestine network of antislavery activists and safe houses that provided refuge for those seeking liberation from slavery. Over the course of approximately 13 perilous missions, she successfully guided around 70 enslaved individuals to safety, including many of her own family members and close friends. Tubman's deep knowledge of the terrain, her resourcefulness, and her unwavering determination allowed her to navigate the dangers of her journeys, often risking her own life to ensure the freedom of others.

Her contributions extended beyond the Underground Railroad; Tubman was also involved in the women's suffrage movement and served as a spy for the Union Army during the Civil War. Her legacy as a courageous leader and advocate for justice continues to inspire generations, highlighting the profound impact one individual can have in the relentless pursuit of equality and human rights. Harriet Tubman's life and work remain a testament to the power of resilience and the enduring fight against oppression.

Who Are the Heroes of Today?

The heroes of today are individuals who are making significant contributions to their communities and the world at large. Through student activism and grassroots movements, they are catalysing national and global change, driven by the dedication and perseverance of principled individuals.

These heroes stand firm in their beliefs, engaging in activism both in their personal lives and in the broader societal context. They create meaningful change by helping others and addressing pressing issues. Today's heroes are those who courageously advocate for the truth, regardless of the consequences, challenging authorities, government agencies, and heads of state. They have risked their lives to confront the injustices faced by African migrants across the globe.

These individuals organize seminars and conferences in various capital cities worldwide to educate Africans and the global community about these critical issues. They are staging protests in cities from New York to Geneva, Brussels to London, raising awareness about the urgent need for change. Our heroes are those who sacrifice their own well-being and that of

their families to ensure that the stories of systematic discrimination and inhumane treatment of African migrants are heard through various media outlets, including print and literature. They are willing to risk everything to share their experiences and struggles during their time in Western societies.

These are the true heroes deserving of recognition in our history. They reside in major cities and villages worldwide, from Johannesburg in South Africa to Nairobi in Kenya, Abuja in Nigeria, Budapest in Hungary, Glasgow in Scotland, and Toronto in Canada, among many others.

We must express our gratitude to our fathers, brothers, and friends who are committed to the fight for a more just society. Notable figures include Patrick Loch Otieno Lumumba, a Kenyan who served as the Director of the Kenya Anti-Corruption Commission; Julius Sello Malema, a prominent South African politician and activist; Ambassador Dr. Arikana Chihombori Quao, a medical doctor and entrepreneur; Dr. Frederick Omoyoma Odorige, a Nigerian writer and human rights activist based in Hungary; Robert Kyagulanyi Ssentamu, also known

as Bobi Wine, a Ugandan politician and singer; and
Omoyele Sowore, a Nigerian human rights activist
and founder of Sahara Reporters.

These individuals represent the spirit of resilience and
determination in the ongoing struggle for justice and
equality.

H.E. Dr. Arikana Chihombori-Quao is a distinguished medical professional whose reputation extends far beyond her clinical expertise. With a profound commitment to health advocacy, she has established herself as a prominent figure in the medical community. Dr. Chihombori-Quao possesses exceptional skills as a public speaker, where her eloquence and passion resonate with diverse audiences, inspiring change and fostering understanding on critical health issues.

In addition to her speaking engagements, she is a dedicated educator, imparting knowledge and empowering future generations of healthcare professionals. Her diplomatic acumen is evident in her ability to navigate complex healthcare policies and collaborate with various stakeholders to promote health equity. As an entrepreneur, she has successfully founded and leads Bell Family Medical Centres in the United States, a role that underscores her commitment to providing accessible and quality healthcare services to underserved populations.

Dr. Chihombori-Quao's journey began in Zimbabwe, where she spent a significant portion of her early life. This experience not only shaped her worldview but also fuelled her passion for improving health outcomes in communities both locally and globally. Today, as the CEO of Bell Family Medical Centres, she continues to make a profound impact on the healthcare landscape, advocating for innovative solutions and holistic approaches to health and wellness. Her work exemplifies a tireless dedication to service, leadership, and the advancement of healthcare for all.

Patrick Loch Otieno Lumumba, born on July 17, 1962, is a distinguished and highly influential figure in Kenya, celebrated for his steadfast dedication to justice, integrity, and the rule of law. His career is marked by a series of impactful roles, notably serving as the Director of the Kenya Anti-Corruption Commission from September 2010 to August 2011. In this capacity, he played a pivotal role in leading the charge against corruption, advocating for systemic reforms that aimed to enhance transparency and accountability within the Kenyan government. His tenure was characterized by a vigorous commitment to ethical governance, which earned him admiration and respect not only within Kenya but also on the international stage.

Since 2014, Lumumba has assumed the esteemed position of Director at The Kenya School of Law, where he has been instrumental in transforming the landscape of legal education in the country. Under his leadership, the institution has embraced innovative teaching methodologies and a curriculum that emphasizes both legal knowledge and ethical practice. Lumumba's vision for legal education is centred on nurturing a new generation of legal professionals who are not only well-versed in the law but also deeply committed to upholding the principles of justice and integrity.

Renowned for his exceptional eloquence and articulate communication style, Lumumba has become a sought-after speaker and commentator on various platforms, including academic conferences, public forums, and media outlets. His ability to convey complex legal concepts in an accessible manner has made him a respected authority in discussions surrounding governance, law, and ethics. Lumumba holds both an LL.B and an LL.M, reflecting his academic excellence and unwavering commitment to the legal profession. Additionally, he is the esteemed Founder of the PLO Lumumba Foundation, an organization dedicated to promoting good governance, ethical leadership, and civic education in Kenya and beyond.

Prof. PLO Lumumba is also recognized as a distinguished alumnus of the Faculty of Law in Kenya, where he laid the groundwork for his illustrious career. His contributions to the legal profession, coupled with his tireless advocacy for ethical leadership, continue to inspire many aspiring lawyers and leaders, solidifying his status as a prominent figure in the ongoing discourse on governance and integrity throughout Africa. Beyond his professional achievements, Prof. PLO Lumumba has emerged as a household name across the African continent. His unwavering commitment to the unity of African nations serves as a clarion call for leaders across the region. He firmly believes that a unified Africa can engage more effectively with Western nations, fostering better relationships and collaborative efforts that benefit the continent as a whole. His vision for a united Africa resonates deeply with many, earning him admiration and affection from countless individuals across the globe.

Prof. Lumumba's enduring legacy is one of hope, inspiration, and a relentless pursuit of justice, making him a beloved figure among Africans and a respected voice in the global conversation on leadership and governance.

Julius Malema, born on March 3, 1981, in Seshego township, South Africa, is a highly regarded South African politician renowned for his impassioned rhetoric and fearless demeanour. He made his foray into national politics as the president of the African National Congress Youth League from 2008 to 2012, subsequently assuming leadership of the Economic Freedom Fighters, a leftist political party he played a pivotal role in establishing in 2013. In 2014, Malema secured a position as a Member of Parliament in the esteemed National Assembly. Raised by his mother, a domestic worker, and his grandmother in what is now the Limpopo province, Malema's early

involvement in political activism can be traced back to his childhood when, at the age of nine, he joined the Masupatsela group, an affiliate of the African National Congress. In 1994, he joined the ANC Youth League, rapidly ascending to prominent local and regional leadership roles within the organization. Malema's commitment to political engagement extended to his involvement in the Congress of South African Students, where he served as the province chairperson in 1997 and subsequently assumed the presidency from 2001 to 2004. In April 2008, he emerged victorious as the president of the ANC Youth League, albeit by a narrow margin, following a contentious group conference.

Dr. Frederick Omoyoma Odorige, born on January 25, 1967, in Delta State, Nigeria, is a distinguished writer and a steadfast advocate for human rights. Currently residing in Hungary, he has established himself as the founder of the esteemed Global Coalition for Security and Democracy in Nigeria, a group registered in Texas, United States. Notably, Dr. Odorige is among the select group of ten Nigerians who have earned a PhD in Military Science. In addition to his professional achievements, he is a devoted father and a courageous individual who consistently speaks truth to power in Nigeria.

Dr. Odorige has become a beacon of hope for many Nigerians living abroad, serving as an advocate for the marginalized and oppressed within Nigeria. I hold him in high esteem for his unwavering commitment to the advancement of our nation.

He is a revered figure for countless individuals.

Robert Kyagulanyi Ssentamu, known widely as Bobi Wine, was born on the 12th of February 1982. He is a highly respected figure in Uganda, known for his contributions as a statesperson, vocalist, and performer. In the past, he held the prestigious role of being a Member of Parliament for the Kyadondo County East constituency in the Wakiso District, situated in the Central Region of Uganda. Furthermore, he currently holds the esteemed position of leading the National Unity Platform political party. Bobi Wine has gained immense popularity and recognition, making him a prominent figure in households across Uganda.

Comrade Omoyele Sowore, born on February 16, 1971, stands out as a prominent figure in the landscape of Nigerian civil society. He is not only a distinguished human rights activist but also a fervent pro-democracy campaigner whose efforts have significantly shaped the discourse surrounding governance and accountability in Nigeria. As a former presidential candidate for the African Action Congress (AAC), Sowore has consistently demonstrated his unwavering commitment to the principles of democracy and social justice.

In addition to his political endeavors, Sowore is the esteemed founder of Sahara Reporters, a pioneering online news agency that has become a vital source of information and investigative journalism in Nigeria. Through this platform, he has played a crucial role in exposing corruption and advocating for transparency within the Nigerian government, thereby empowering citizens with the knowledge necessary to hold their leaders accountable.

Sowore is also the visionary behind two impactful movements: Revolution Now and Take It Back. These initiatives have galvanized a significant portion of the Nigerian populace, urging them to reclaim their nation from the grips of misgovernance and societal injustices. His ability to mobilize and inspire young Nigerians reflects his deep understanding of the socio-political landscape and his commitment to fostering a new generation of leaders.

As a preeminent advocate within the Nigerian political sphere, Sowore has earned immense respect and admiration from both his peers and the general public. His relentless pursuit of a better Nigeria resonates with many, and his calls for reform and civic engagement have sparked a renewed sense of hope among citizens.

Despite his significant contributions and the passion he brings to his activism, it is a sobering reality that this youthful and dynamic leader may never have the opportunity to govern Nigeria. Nevertheless, Nigerians will undoubtedly remain eternally grateful for his tireless efforts and unwavering dedication to the cause of democracy and human rights, recognizing him as a beacon of hope in their ongoing struggle for a just and equitable society.

Chief (Dr.) Patrick Osagie Eholor, also known as Ultimate Equal, is a renowned Nigerian/Canadian Human Rights Activist and the creator of the 'Mind is Ultimate' idea. He is recognized as the father of Nigerian students.

Dr. Patrick was born on 24th December 1964 into the family of Palmer Osagie Eholor in Benin City, specifically in the Ovia Northeast Local Government Area of Edo state. He grew up in an average family, with his parents working as traders.

From an early age, Chief Patrick displayed a strong determination to succeed. He recalls a pivotal moment in his early days when his father had to make him choose between Christmas attire and attending school.

Before relocating to Canada, Dr. Patrick engaged in

various odd jobs, such as selling newspapers and kerosene, to support himself and further his education.

Despite facing numerous challenges as a teenager,

he resisted peer pressure and drew inspiration from great minds such as Martin Luther King Jr., Eleanor Roosevelt, Nelson Mandela, Malcolm X, and

Ransome Fela Kuti. He describes them as unique, genuine, sincere, and natural, considering them to be intellectual treasures that Nigeria has lost.

Having studied Sociology at Humber College in Etobicoke, Canada, Dr. Patrick is a social crusader who is dedicated to transforming Nigeria into a model state. He is known for his boldness and bravery and has taken individual actions that have benefited society. In the year 2000, he founded the One Love Family and Caring Association (One Love Foundation, Nigeria), a non-profit/non-governmental organization, to promote his philanthropic ideals.

Chief Dr. Patrick Eholor, also known as Ultimate Equal, is renowned for his advocacy of equal rights and justice. Recently awarded a Doctorate in humanity, he has been actively involved in public interest initiatives for the past 25 years.

CHAPTER NINETEEN
RECOMMENDATIONS

Here are some recommendations from the authors for addressing systemic racism, discrimination, and human rights violations against Africans and people of African descent. I propose a four-point agenda:

STEP UP: Acknowledge and dismantle discriminatory laws.

PURSUIT OF JUSTICE: End impunity and foster trust within communities of African origin.

LISTEN: Ensure that the voices of people of African descent are heard and their opinions respected.

REDRESS: Address historical injustices, implement extraordinary measures, and provide restorative justice.

ALL MIGRANTS ARE UNDER SIEGE

The United Kingdom, Canada, and the United States are perceived as hospitable and welcoming to migrants.

A significant majority of the foreign-born population (72%) believe that the UK is a welcoming place for

migrants, and 91% feel that challenging work enables migrants to succeed. Overall, perceptions of the UK

among the foreign-born population are positive. During the period from 2015 to 2017, three-quarters (72%) expressed that the UK is hospitable or welcoming to individuals from their countries of origin, while 91% believed that migrants can achieve success through challenging work.

Famous Quotes from the Author:

The sole instrument I possess in my struggle against those who have chosen to align themselves with my oppressor is the power of my writing. It serves as my voice, my shield, and my means of resistance. This form of expression is not merely a pastime; it is a profound extension of my identity and my convictions. No one can strip me of this ability, for it is deeply rooted in my spirit and my determination to advocate for truth and justice. Through the written word, I can articulate my thoughts, share my experiences, and challenge the narratives imposed upon me. It is a weapon that cannot be confiscated or silenced, and I wield it with unwavering resolve.

Second quote:

Let it be known to all mankind that even in the twilight of my existence, as I lie upon my deathbed, I remain

resolute in my intention to articulate the most significant truths and values that I wish to be remembered for. It is in these final moments, when the weight of my experiences and the essence of my character converge, that I find it imperative to pen down the critical thoughts and profound insights that have shaped my life. I aspire for these words to resonate beyond my passing, serving as a testament to my beliefs, aspirations, and the legacy I hope to leave behind. In this act of writing, I seek not only to convey my innermost convictions but also to inspire future generations to reflect upon the principles that have guided me throughout my journey.

THE END

Explore a diverse collection of thought-provoking works by the author, each offering unique insights and narratives that resonate with readers. Among these titles is "The Sojourn of an African Child," a poignant exploration of childhood experiences against the backdrop of African culture. Delve into "The Refugee Project," which sheds light on the struggles and resilience of displaced individuals seeking a new life.

"Migrants Under Siege," the author tackles the pressing issues faced by migrants in today's world, while "Ungrateful Friends" examines the complexities of relationships and loyalty. "Crime and Criminality Expose" provides a critical analysis of societal issues related to crime, offering a compelling perspective on justice and morality.

Additionally, "The Secret" invites readers to uncover hidden truths, while "Broken Genealogy" delves into the intricacies of family history and identity. For those seeking practical guidance, "A Step-by-Step Approach to Legal Emigration from Africa" serves as

an invaluable resource for navigating the challenges of relocation.

The author also highlights the essential qualities of remarkable women in "Identifying the Qualities of Admirable Women," celebrating their contributions and influence. "My Ghost Will Haunt You," readers are taken on a haunting journey that blends the supernatural with personal reflection. Finally, "Who Among them truly Deserves Recognition?" prompts readers to consider the criteria for acknowledgment and appreciation in our society.

Each of these titles offers a unique lens through which to view the world, making them essential additions to any reader's library.